Weapons For The Battlefield

Jean Mallory

Copyright 2011 © by Jean Mallory

©All rights reserved. This book and its entire contents may not be reproduced, in any form for any purpose without the prior written consent of the publishers or author.

First edition

Cover: The cover was designed by Kaitlyn Reiter.

Some of the events in this book are based on true experiences and situations. When applicable, names and situations have been changed. The majority of the characters and events portrayed are fictitious, and any resemblance to incidents, or persons, living or dead is purely coincidental.

All Scripture quotations are taken from:
The Holy Bible
King James Version

ISBN: 978-1-84961-132-9
RealTime Publishing
Limerick, Ireland

Dedication

Unto him that loved us, and washed us from our sins in his own blood, Revelations 1:5b

Acknowledgements

Thank you to a dear friend and author, Janet Nicolet, for her help and prayers whenever I called for advice.

Thank you to a wonderful prayer warrior and friend, Bernice (Granny) Riley, who walked with me and prayed with me as I personally learned about the 'Weapons for the Battlefield.'

Thank you to the Digital Design class at Haney Technical Center, instructor Jason Heath

Special thanks to my editors:
Pastor T.A. Green
Karen Leach
Dave Hanson

Contents

Dedication	3
Acknowledgements	4
Contents	5
Preface	7
1. The Necessity of the Battle	9
She Just Wanted To Help	15
A Wake Up Call	17
Just Being Sociable	19
I'll Fix It First	21
Keep On Fighting	23
He Lost the Battle	25
2. Being Prepared for the Battle	28
It's Just Not Right	33
If We Had Known	36
Chaos	39
Crybaby	42
3. The Whole Armor	44
Surrendering All	48
The Armor of the Word	51
Stand	53
Provoked	56
Contending	59
4. Loins Girt About With Truth	62
Carried by the Unseen Hand	66
Real or Counterfeit	69
The Truth Carries Us	71
Overwhelmed	74
Knowing God's Will	76
5. Breastplate of Righteousness	78
Righteousness Goes With You	82
Continuing On	84
Distractions	88
Setting an Example	90

6. Feet Shod with the Preparation of the Gospel of Peace	92
The Boots	96
A Shattered Life	98
Locked Out	100
Irritation	103
Change of Plans	105
7. Shield of Faith	107
Only Believe	113
Communication Broken	115
In the Midst of It All	117
Lies	119
8. Helmet of Salvation	122
There Must Be an Order	124
Beauty in the Midst	126
He Must Increase	128
Silent Struggle	131
9. Sword of the Spirit	134
The Word Is Vital	138
Regrets	141
Giving All	143
Offended: Satan's Trap	145
10. Prayer and Supplication	150
Return From the Battle	152
Persecution	154
Praying Always	156
Mysteries of God	158
11. On the Run	160
Authors Note	172

Preface

There is no question that we face many battles in our lives. As we move closer to the end time, it seems that the battles become more devastating and harder to fight. The Christian used to go from valley to victorious mountaintop before another battlefield in the valley found us fighting again.

Now the battles seem much more numerous and we often go from battle to battle with little rest in between. This speaks to me of just how close we are to the Lord's return. Satan is fighting with all the tricks he knows to defeat as many as possible.

The continued fighting can be devastating when there is little rest between the battles. The toll on our physical and mental strength is difficult. It helps to know we don't fight alone and God has provided weapons suitable for us to fight with.

He knew we would face many difficulties in this life. As we read the Word of God, we realize throughout the entire Bible that people faced struggles in their determination to follow Him and live a Godly life.

When I was a very small girl, I remember being in a crowd of people and my mother telling me to hold tight to her hand and to not let go. Somehow in a moment of distraction, I lost hold of that hand. She must have also been distracted to let go of that little hand that reached up to her.

Panic filled my thoughts when I realized my mother was no longer there. Frantically, I reached and sought the safety of that hand. Oh, the relief that I felt when once again I found a hand above mine to grasp. But then, something was wrong. I looked up into the face of a total stranger who in bewilderment gazed at me wondering who I was and where I came from.

The panic and fear consumed me again, as I snatched my hand away. Now sobbing hysterically, I just stood there as the reality set in that I was alone in that terrifying crowd. In a few moments, my frantic mother found and comforted me.

Although I was very small, I'll never forget the terror of that moment when I was lost. It's the way every Christian should feel when they move away from the safety and protection of Jesus.

When we face our trials and battles lightly without the proper weapons, we can also become lost. Wandering around half-prepared, we don't realize the seriousness of each fight. We face the risk of being overcome and defeated by the enemy. There is nothing more terrifying than being alone, lost without Christ in the midst of the enemy's territory.

Ephesians 6:10-18 - Nine verses that give spiritual battlefield instructions. They are important and vital to the believer in fighting spiritual battles. They describe the character of the enemy and what must be done to counteract his deception. They begin by describing the armour that must be used to be victorious and end with an urgent call to persevere in prayer which is an essential part of the conflict.

Christians must not only use the proper weapons, but also stand and fight, never turning away. Our hand must remain constantly in the hand of the One who holds the keys to victory. It's true we will lose some of the skirmishes, but we will win the victory in the end.

~~~

*Books written by Jean Mallory are available as paperback at www.amazon.com or in ebook form at http://store.theebooksale.com. Books are also available by request at most bookstores.

Chapter One

The Necessity of the Battle

Christians fight spiritual battles. It was necessary in the Old Testament times for the people of God to fight physical battles.

Nehemiah told, while rebuilding the wall, how they fought with one hand and built with the other.

Nehemiah 4:17,18 They which builded on the wall, and they that bare burdens, with those that laded, every one with one of his hands wrought in the work, and with the other hand held a weapon.

For the builders, every one had his sword girded by his side, and so builded. And he that sounded the trumpet was by me.

We don't usually have hand-to-hand combat now, but spiritual battles can be very difficult. Often the enemy is not seen, just his agents or situations created by him.

Sometimes the warfare is hot and heavy involving every circumstance imaginable. Satan has a very short time left here on this Earth. He's working extremely hard to pull people away from Christ. The attacks are more intense. They are fiercer and closer together. The end- time is approaching, very, very, soon.

Satan will not turn loose and give in, even though he knows his fate is sealed. He will tempt and work very hard to deceive and cause Christians to stumble and fall. Never forget the kind of battle that the Christian faces, as well as the kinds of weapons available.

2 Corinthians 10:3,4 For though we walk in the flesh, we do not war after the flesh:
(For the weapons of our warfare are not carnal, but mighty through God to the pulling down of strong holds;)

Why should we fight battles, anyway? Can't we just live in this world and share Christ by loving everyone and living in peace? By our actions and words, couldn't we show that God is a loving God that cares for us and just wants us to back away from conflict and be gentle? It's an attractive theory, but it really doesn't work that way. The believer must take a positive, firm stand, believing God's Word, and hating the sin that dominates this evil world.

Exodus 11:7 ... that ye may know how that the LORD doth put a difference between the Egyptians and Israel.

This is one of many scriptures that tell us there is a difference between the children of God and the children of this world.
Sometimes we treat fighting as an option. It is not! We think it is avoidable. It is not! We are called to be soldiers.

2 Timothy 2:3,4 Thou therefore endure hardness, as a good soldier of Jesus Christ.
No man that warreth entangleth himself with the affairs of this life; that he may please him who hath chosen him to be a soldier.

This world is evil, depraved, and it is becoming more ungodly every day. Satan doesn't take any time off. We can end the day, go to bed and sleep, but he's right back fighting against us when we get up. Don't take him lightly! Don't make jokes about him or his power. The devil is real. He is hostile, active, and smart.

1 Peter 5:8 Be sober, be vigilant; because your adversary the devil, as a roaring lion, walketh about, seeking whom he may devour:

Soberness and seriousness are often qualities that we lack. We like to 'make light of things.' We joke often about things we should not joke about, not realizing we are playing right into the enemy's hands. How much safer it would be if he were just a lion. A lion that we could see and hear and guard against.

One reason we often don't recognize him and his filthy tactics is because he is a liar. Always appearing where we would never think he would be: with other Christians, in church, in the pulpit, in our family, on the pew next to us. Jesus had to rebuke his own disciple. ***Mark 8:33***.

Satan is real. He is sly, devious, and constantly prowling to come at us in any area that we are not protected. One of our worst faults is criticism of others. That is exactly what Satan does. Remember that the next time you decide to criticize. That unkind, critical word almost always returns to the one who was talked about, and causes more trouble.

Sitting back and not standing for what is right is just what Satan wants us to do.

We become accepting of worldly practices. Then, even worse, we begin to participate. Just a little at first, saying, "Well that's not really so bad." But then, more and more, we become identical to all the evil the world has to offer. We become just like the world and how the scripture about coming out from the world and being separate doesn't apply anymore.

2 Corinthians 6:17-18 Wherefore come out from among them, and be ye separate, saith the Lord, and touch not the unclean thing; and I will receive you,
And will be a Father unto you, and ye shall be my sons and daughters, saith the Lord Almighty.

Fighting spiritual battles defines who we are and what side we are on. With every battle Christians have a choice. We can give in to the attack, take the easy way, and surrender to his insidious demands, or we can follow Christ in His leading, resisting, fighting, and standing for the right in every situation.

We must fight in these battles and not give in to the enemy. Our very lives depend on it. Each battle or skirmish that the enemy wins leaves us weaker and depleted of more strength. Each battle we win will leave us stronger and more likely to finish our course and be victorious at the end.

What kind of Christian do you want to be? A strong, competent one, that depends on Christ to win every battle? Or one that becomes weaker with every confrontation, as Satan gains a foothold in your life by winning these seemingly endless skirmishes?

Will you finally give in completely and turn away from Christ as every element of this world takes over your very being, and you no longer even pretend to live for Christ?

Zephaniah 1:6 And them that are turned back from the LORD; and those that have not sought the LORD, nor enquired for him.

2 Peter 2:20 For if after they have escaped the pollutions of the world through the knowledge of the Lord and Saviour Jesus Christ, they are again entangled therein, and overcome, the latter end is worse with them than the beginning.

The key to surviving these battles is fighting in the Lord's power instead of our own strength.

Ephesians 6:10 tells us ***Finally, my brethren, be strong in the Lord and in the power of His might.***

The Christian life cannot be lived without a spiritual battle. The intensity increases as the end-time approaches. To be strong in the Lord is to be made powerful in Him.

The Ephesians would have understood just what Paul was speaking of. The power of <u>His</u> might would have been the same power that raised Jesus from the dead! It's the same power that saved them when they were dead in sin. And now that same power is available to Christians to fight spiritual battles. It is completely sufficient.

Acts 9:22 But Saul increased the more in strength, and confounded the Jews which dwelt at Damascus, proving that this is very Christ.

Spiritual strength is not like physical strength. It doesn't matter how many vitamins you take, or how you eat, exercise, or work out. A Christian cannot strengthen himself spiritually. He must be empowered by another. The Lord Jesus is our strength. It can never be just a one-time turning to Him for help, but a constant, ongoing calling on Him and depending on his strength.

'In the Lord' speaks of a life lived very closely united with Him and being assured of victory in Him.

1 John 2:14 I have written unto you, fathers, because ye have known him that is from the beginning. I have written unto you, young men, because ye are strong, and

the word of God abideth in you, and ye have overcome the wicked one.

It is necessary to fight hard, using the weapons the Lord has provided for us. Just an occasional, "Get thee behind me, Satan", or prayer for strength is not enough. It should be a daily way of life for the Christian. As the battles rage, we must continue to fight.

She Just Wanted To Help

Carrie watched the eggs with fascination. They were beginning to hatch, and she could see the cracks and hear the baby chicks as they started to struggle to peck their way through the eggs.

All morning, she ran back to the henhouse every few minutes to check on the progress. Finally she became worried that they just couldn't find their way out by themselves. The mama chicken had pecked a hole in the ends of the egg, and she clucked encouragement at the babies while she kept them warm.

The baby chicks would squirm and peck a while, then rest a long time before trying again. Carrie decided that they probably needed more help to break out of the shell. She gently helped the cracks to enlarge and make a way out, and then she peeled off the sections of shell from the chicks.

Carrie's mom found her in the henhouse when it was time for lunch. "Oh, Carrie, I don't think you should help them." In the coming hours, Carrie realized that she shouldn't have helped at all. Most of the little chicks died.
Carrie was so sad. Her mom comforted her and explained about the natural process of the egg-hatching.

"The chicks need that struggle and the time it takes to prepare them for the exertion of living outside of the shell. The long resting times were necessary for recovery and for the babies to absorb the nutrients in the yolk. It's necessary that they absorb all of the nutrients available to make them strong enough to live independently."

~~~

It's also necessary for us to struggle as we pass through the many obstacles placed in our pathway as we traverse through this life. Each struggle and every conflict prepares us for that harder fight that is just ahead. The mama chicken tried to help by pecking a hole just in the end of the egg and clucking to encourage them, and also by keeping them warm.

Our Savior always tries to help us by being there and giving just enough encouragement and support to urge us to fight on and finish the struggle on our own. He knows we will be made stronger by each conflict. He knows what is ahead for us and just how strong we must be to complete each battle and prepare us for that final victory ahead.

1 Corinthians 6:19,20 What? know ye not that your body is the temple of the Holy Ghost which is in you, which ye have of God, and ye are not your own?
For ye are bought with a price: therefore glorify God in your body, and in your spirit, which are God's.

Wake Up Call

Amy, the night manager of the small convenience store, gathered the last of the smashed grocery boxes and headed out to make the final trip to the dumpster for the evening.

She was tired. It was stock day and there were only two people working to get all the stock on the shelves before the day was over. It was a difficult, physical task. Still ahead, before the midnight closing was the exhausting job of mopping the floors and the other regular nightly chores.

The dumpster was located at the far end of the store. It was dark in that area, and as she approached with her arms full, she didn't see the dark form running towards her.

Suddenly she was sprawled on the asphalt when he tackled her. Pure survival instinct caused her to twist away and get up screaming and kicking. He was slim, and not much taller than she was. Praying for God's help, she hit him with all her strength and continued to scream and yell. Her assailant took off running full speed into the woods near the store.

Delores, the other clerk, came running out of the store, along with the only customer who had been inside.

"Amy? You OK? What happened?" Delores pulled her towards the lighted front of the store.

Amy answered, "Yes, I guess so. I'm just all scraped up." She recounted what had occurred.

"Oh Amy, I think I would have been too scared to fight I think I would have just cried and begged him not to hurt me."

We all react in different ways. Amy fought back; Delores would have cried and asked for mercy. When the enemy of our soul comes against us, what is our reaction? It might be a physical battle, or it could be a stress-filled attack against our mind.

Satan would love for you to cry out to him for mercy. The only mercy he knows is to send people to an everlasting, burning torment. The only chance for survival we have is to fight with all our strength, depending on the weapons God has provided.

What if Amy had not fought? It was late, dark, and no one was around that side of the store. Would she have been beaten? Raped? Murdered? Would it have been too late by the time Delores noticed she was missing and go to find her? Perhaps Delores would have been a victim, also.

Psalm 140:7   O GOD the Lord, the strength of my salvation, thou hast covered my head in the day of battle.

We fight in the battles, but God gives us strength, and is with us in the fight. Things don't always turn out well in the battles, but we have the peace and assurance that we are in the will of God, and He is with us.

Just Being Sociable

Greg offered a beer to Scott after the softball game at the company picnic. "Look at that, they didn't spare any expense with the amenities this year. Last year they just bought the cheap stuff."

"No thanks, Greg. I'll just get one of the sodas," Scott replied.

"Oh, no," Greg groaned. "Don't tell me you don't even drink socially just to be part of the crowd? I know you go to church all the time, and don't curse or even go to the movies. But what will just one little beer hurt? You know, just to fit in with everyone else. People really think you're strange, you know."

Scott laughed, "Well, I guess I am strange according to most worldly standards. The Bible says to be separate from the world. It's really not difficult to do that with Jesus in my life.

"I was a part of all that before I asked Jesus to turn my life around. In fact I drank to excess, and partied constantly, but it destroyed my home, my career and my health. Between the expense and the constant hangovers, there was no time left for the really important things like my wife, my children, and working hard to provide for them.

"That's why I'm working here, starting at the bottom all over again. Perhaps one day my family will realize there really has been a change and allow me back in their lives," Scott went on.

"I just don't see how one little beer will harm anything," Greg retorted, "It's not like we're in a bar or anything."

"That's exactly the way I used to feel, Greg, but it's different now. There's a different set of values built into me, and I know even one beer could destroy my testimony for the Lord. I really do have to remain separate in everything I do. There is nothing to compare to the peace in my heart and the clean feeling I have living for Christ. One beer would start the rollercoaster all over again."

~~~

In ***Genesis 1:2-4,*** the Word says: ***And the earth was without form, and void; and darkness was upon the face of the deep. And the Spirit of God moved upon the face of the waters.***
And God said, Let there be light: and there was light.
And God saw the light, that it was good: and God divided the light from the darkness.

God said the light was good. He never said the darkness was good. He separated the light from the darkness. It's necessary for those that would follow Christ to separate themselves from the things of the darkness.

In the darkness, Christians can lose their way and follow after the wrong things. Only in the LIGHT can they see what truly is good and what is not.

2 Corinthians 6:17 Wherefore come out from among them, and be ye separate, saith the Lord, and touch not the unclean thing; and I will receive you.

I'll Fix It First

Patricia shook her head sadly as they left the funeral home. "It's just so sad, David. I know how much you loved your sister, but it breaks my heart that she never could turn her back on sin and accept Christ into her life."

"I know, Honey," David answered. "She was never a really bad person, but we're all sinners, and until we make that decision, there is no hope of eternal life. I remember her always saying, 'I will become a Christian, but not right now.' There always seemed to be something more important at the moment than for her to leave that life of sin behind.

"She said we seemed to have more struggles and battles than she did, but she never realized there's no need to fight Satan if he has control of you. I could never make her realize that we never fight a battle alone, and we know what the outcome of the war will be. These Earthly struggles are just temporary in light of eternal life."

As they entered the car, Patricia said, "I wonder if she really thought she would be OK, since she was basically a 'good person', at least by the standards of the world. She smoked and drank a little, and told a few lies, but never really broke the law or anything.

"She was always telling me that she would get saved as soon as she fixed a few things in her life. But we're never really able to fix them ourselves." David wiped a tear from his cheek. "That wreck was so unexpected; the bus driver had a heart attack and smashed into her little car."

Patricia turned to him and grasped his hand. "We don't know what might have happened in that car before she died. She could have repented and called out to Jesus to come into her heart. Many have done that when they realize there is no time left."

"You're right, Honey, but it's a sobering lesson for those that let other things get in the way and don't turn to the Lord in time. She could have been saved. Perhaps we will know when we get to Heaven."

~~~

Exodus 12:33-34 And the Egyptians were urgent upon the people, that they might send them out of the land in haste; for they said, We be all dead men.
And the people took their dough before it was leavened, their kneading troughs being bound up in their clothes upon their shoulders.

Often there is a haste involved in following Jesus. Leavening was a symbol of sin in the Old Testament. When the Egyptians finally let the Israelites leave, they wanted them to go quickly, as they feared for their very lives.

The Israelites did leave quickly; they took the dough before it was leavened. They didn't worry at that point what they were leaving behind. They knew their only chance for life involved leaving. If they had remained, they would have been slaves to the Egyptians forever.

Those who never accept Jesus are also slaves. Slaves to their so-called freedom, but actually that freedom is what binds them and keeps them tied to what Satan wants for their lives.

Only by accepting Jesus into their lives can true freedom be found.

Keep On Fighting

Allie shifted her weight on the uncomfortable hospital bed again, trying to find a better position, but there didn't seem to be one.

"Hi, Allie", said her neighbor and friend, Julie, as she came through the door and sat in the bedside chair. "Are you feeling better today?" Not waiting for an answer, Julie went on talking. "I fed the cat and watered your plants. The mail was just advertisements, so I didn't bring them."

"I am feeling some better, in fact the doctor said if I had some help at home, he would consider letting me be discharged. But I guess there's not much chance of that. I just can't afford to hire someone. I know you would help, Julie, but it's just too much for you to handle alone."

"What about Sally? Can't she help at all?" Julie answered. "I know she doesn't have much to do with you, but she is your daughter."

"Well, she said I could go to their house and have Missy's room, but I really don't want to put her out. Sally just hates my Christian life, and really doesn't want me around. I've prayed for her for so many years, but it seems like she'll never forgive me for the past problems."

Allie's voice broke, and tears slipped down her cheeks. "I get so tired of fighting in these battles, Julie. It hurts so much when it's your loved ones, and they just seem to hate you."

"We don't get to leave the battlefield in this life," Julie answered gently. "The reason our loved ones seem to hate our lives is because they are under strong conviction, and deep down they know they need to turn their lives over to God. As long as we are breathing, the enemy will try to pull us down and draw us back into his realm, which is the world.

"The best we can do is to remember where our strength lies, and remember that these battles are but a small thing. They are a small price to pay compared to the price Jesus paid for our salvation. The enemy knows what a threat we are to him, and how we pray for our loved ones. He knows many will be saved because of those prayers. We must fight on, dear friend, as long as there is breath in our bodies. We must continue to fight."

~~~

Acts 20:24 But none of these things move me, neither count I my life dear unto myself, so that I might finish my course with joy, and the ministry, which I have received of the Lord Jesus, to testify the gospel of the grace of God.

Paul spoke of finishing his course with **joy** and **continuing** to minister the gospel. He faced so many problems, afflictions, and a tremendous amount of opposition. He was often in jail, bound, shipwrecked, and hated.

It is necessary to keep on and complete this earthly battle we find ourselves in. As long as we are ministering the gospel, even in the midst of numerous battlefields, we will finish our course with joy.

He Lost the Battle

The faces in the congregation first expressed curiosity, then surprise, and finally shock when the board member took the platform and quietly informed them that Pastor Williams had been asked to resign and Brother Mills would bring a message this morning.

He then asked for applicants to apply for the job of church secretary as quickly as possible to fill in the vacancy. The pew where the pastor's wife and small child usually sat was conspicuously vacant. The congregation knew the older children were probably not in the back of the church in the children's service, either. The church secretary was not in the sanctuary.

Old Brother Mills did his best, but obviously did not have much time to prepare. It was a short service, and it seemed everyone had their minds elsewhere.

As the people filed out silently, many of the group reflected on the past few months, and knew that the vague rumors that had been circulating were accurate concerning the Pastor and the pretty Secretary.

Many shed tears as they remembered what a strong prayer warrior the Pastor had always been, how many crises he had helped them through, and how much they had depended on him.

The coming months were stormy in the little church. Some just could not recover, thinking that if the Pastor could succumb to the wiles of Satan, how could they ever make it without falling?

Some of the people left the church and didn't bother to find another. Those that were left couldn't agree on a new Pastor. They doubted that any would ever be able to stand and lead them and be able to fight the necessary battles.

Brother Mills became a source of strength to those remaining in the church. His years of experience and Bible knowledge helped them to stay strong. When asked, "How could it have happened to such a strong Pastor, who knew the Word and had fought so many spiritual battles valiantly?" he replied, "The fight is continual; you can't quit fighting, and you can't take vacations from the battles if you intend to make it."

~~~

David let down his guard and stepped back from the fight. As king, he lived a life of luxury and self-indulgence. He enjoyed these pleasures and became soft. He never intended to sin and grieve the Lord, but like all of us, he was weak in some areas and he quit the fight.

2 Samuel 11:1 And it came to pass, after the year was expired, at the time when kings go forth to battle, that David sent Joab, and his servants with him, and all Israel; and they destroyed the children of Ammon, and besieged Rabbah. But David tarried still at Jerusalem.

The rest of chapter 11 records the sin of David with Bathsheba and the murder of Uriah. His weakness resulted in sin and death. The fight is ongoing. We can never let down our guard and step back from the battle. David's place was in the midst of the fight, not relaxing at the palace.

None are exempt from fighting, not even a man after God's own heart. He gave into temptation, and then to lustful desire, then to murder. Temptation was not a sin, even Jesus was tempted, <u>but</u> without sin. Temptation is to show us what is in us. God already knows, but we often don't. When faced with temptation, we will either fight harder or we might fall. Our daily prayer should be not to be led into temptation.

This chapter is a warning to all believers about the necessity of the battle. David fell from that place of grace.

Galatians 5:4 Christ is become of no effect unto you, whosoever of you are justified by the law; ye are fallen from grace.

All are vulnerable when we become too lazy to fight in the battle and let our guard down.

1 Corinthians 10:12 Wherefore let him that thinketh he standeth take heed lest he fall.

Chapter Two

Being Prepared for the Battle

Ephesians 6:12 For we wrestle not against flesh and blood, but against principalities, against powers, against the rulers of the darkness of this world, against spiritual wickedness in high places.

If you could describe the spiritual battlefield of the Christian, what words would you use? Perhaps words like invisible, dark, evil, Satanic? Actually, our vocabulary doesn't even contain words to describe the horrible powers that we face spiritually.

We fight a bloody and lasting war as Christians. Wrestling conveys the personal nature of the conflict. We face not only deceptiveness, but brute strength.

Wrestling is a hand-to-hand, solitary, combative encounter. It's not a team sport. Instead, it's very personal and is fought one-on-one. Satan loves to get you alone and intimidate you. Always wrestle with God standing beside you. Invite Him by prayer to be with you.

In wrestling, you can feel the hot breath of your opponent in your face. In the professional entertainment field, wrestling has a reputation for underhanded, unfair tactics. Blood and suffering seem to be part of the sport.

No wonder God provides weapons to fight this war. It seems to be a much more difficult struggle when we fight against forces that are not physical.

It often seems like we really are battling flesh and blood. Satan moves in close for the fight. The soldier is not dodging bullets from a distance, but instead the enemy is grappling with your flesh. It appears that our adversary is in human form. The human instruments he uses are certainly real. But Satan is the power that is working behind them.

We actually face an enemy that we cannot see! It is a devious, demonic power that uses those we are familiar with, those that we can see, hear and touch.

Even though we can't see him, it doesn't make him less real. Before repenting and accepting Christ, people are guided by Satan. ***Ephesians 2:2***. He has a very active influence over sinners. Paul called him the god of this world, blinding sinners to the truth, ***2 Corinthians 4:4***. After salvation, Christians are in complete conflict with him and his evil army.

The goal of wrestling is to throw your opponent to the ground and then hold him down for the time required. The ancient wrestlers anointed themselves with oil to be slippery when their opponent tried to pin them.

The Christian can pray and also be anointed with the oil that comes from above. The enemy won't stand a chance. He cannot hurt what is holy.

When you are triumphant over sin or temptation, the enemy is down. Keep resisting and fighting! Make sure he is on his back, and hold him for the defeat. God says sin has to die and not live.

If another battle appears and tries to defeat you again, you might get discouraged. You might wonder why this is happening. Gideon thought the same.

And Gideon said unto him, Oh my Lord, if the LORD be with us, why then is all this befallen us? and where be all his miracles which our fathers told us of, saying, Did not the LORD bring us up from Egypt? but now the LORD hath forsaken us, and delivered us into the hands of the Midianites. Judges 6:13.

Remember, we are called to be soldiers and warriors, not conquerors. Jesus is the conqueror. We do win individual battles, but only with Him beside us directing the fight. Our struggle is human, and proves that the two natures exist within us, and they will until we reach that place of rest reserved for us. There is a reason and a purpose for our struggle. The reward is the heavenly home and a permanent crown.

Satan is called an Angel of Light in *2 Corinthians 11:14.* What a deceiver, never showing his true face. He controls those that do not know Christ, making sin look attractive.

We must keep our attention on the power behind the things that we face. It's not the people, the situations or groups that come against us, but the power behind them. Satan is a spirit, an actual being that hinders and attacks. He can and will interrupt your prayer life, keep you from reading the Bible, and do everything he can to keep you out of church.

The enemy presents a well-organized force working against us. He uses neighbors, employers, friends, sons, and daughters. The devil is not omnipresent, omniscient, or omnipotent.

He cannot be everywhere at once, so he uses all of those whom he controls. He does not have unlimited power or authority to take our lives. Neither does he know all things. These are attributes of God alone.

He does have a large group, even a kingdom, you could say. A kingdom of demonic forces, those who will obey him, whom he can use to further his will. He also has control over those who are not committed to Christ.

Perhaps his most powerful weapon against us is to bring mental oppression, which leads to depression and discouragement. He is a liar and will stoop to any level to bring feelings of 'Oh, poor me' against our minds.

In *Revelation 12:10*, Satan is called the accuser of the brethren. In *1 Thessalonians 3:5*, Paul calls him a tempter. He is also called a thief who steals the Word that was sown into hearts in *Matthew 4:15.*

Spiritual wickedness in high places is a well-organized force working against us. The enemy doesn't take vacations, he is constantly working to steal, kill, and destroy.

We must be prepared at all times by knowing the Word of God and relying on His protection when this demonic force raises his power against us.

All Christians wrestle spiritually. The battle does not exempt any Christians, including pastors, teachers, and those with other ministries. The battle will continue until we reach heaven. Paul wrote to the Thessalonians that he would have come sooner, but he was hindered by Satan. *1 Thessalonians 2:18*

In the midst of the battle we must remember who wins the victory. We must remember that we don't fight alone.

Exodus 14:19, 20 And the angel of God, which went before the camp of Israel, removed and went behind them; and the pillar of the cloud went from before their face, and stood behind them:
And it came between the camp of the Egyptians and the camp of Israel; and it was a cloud and darkness to them, but it gave light by night to these: so that the one came not near the other all the night.

When the Egyptians approached the Israelites from the rear, intent upon destroying them, God removed the pillar of cloud from the front and put it behind them. The Egyptians could not see through it, and the Israelites were protected the entire night.

When the battle is strong, and we feel the enemy approaching and breathing down our necks, remember: GOD HAS OUR BACKS! He not only leads the way, but

He protects our unprotected backside, becoming a cloud of darkness to the world, but giving light to his children.

In that darkest battle, when you see no end or victory in sight, no reconciliation possible, and no conclusion to the matter, God knows and can see the end. He knows the victory, the reconciliation, and the conclusion. He is working even in this! You are not alone.

God won that battle between the Egyptians and the Israelites. He kept his children safe. All the Egyptians drowned in the Red Sea, while the Israelites walked upon dry ground.

We want the enemy destroyed. We don't want those loved ones that he is using to be destroyed. We want God to save them. God can take care of that, too.

God said to follow Him. He said I'll provide guidance and direction. He also said I'll protect your front and your vulnerable back. In everything we must trust Him. When we are overwhelmed, there are two places of safety for the soldier. The first is always the name of Jesus. In His name there is victory. Call upon Him often. The second place of safety is in the promises located in His Word. They are placed there for encouragement, for renewing our strength and for help whenever needed.

It's Just Not Right

Ben entered the church office, right on time for his appointment with the pastor. Tina looked up and said "Hi, Mr. Stephens, I'll tell Pastor Davis that you're here."

"Ben, it's good to see you. I always miss you when you don't make it to the services."

"Yes, and that seems it's more and more often. That's kind of what I need to talk to you about. Did you know I accepted another large promotion last year with the company?" Ben asked the pastor.

"I do know that you're doing really well in your career, Ben. Aren't you Second Vice President now?"

"Yes," Ben answered, "It's one of those companies that profits tremendously when the economy and most things are really suffering. That really doesn't seem right. When I accept the large bonuses, I feel that I'm agreeing with what they are doing. It's perfectly legal, but it just doesn't seem right. It seems to me to be unfair to the poorer people.

"They provide me with larger and larger bonuses, but there is a lot of travel and being away from home. Our lifestyle has increased along with the raises and bonuses, but my conscience torments me.

"I know most people are tightening belts and barely getting by. So many people have lost their jobs. If they just didn't give me such huge bonuses twice a year. My boss and the others say I'm crazy, and I should be glad for it. I know all the other companies like ours do the same thing, and people don't think anything of it, but taking that money almost seems like I'm contributing to all the problems of society right now.

"The people I work with just close their eyes as to where the profits come from and grab the money. My friends tell me to just give it away if I don't want it, but that doesn't seem to be the point.

"I feel more and more that the company shouldn't even be making a profit when times are bad. It seems wrong, even though in this line of business everyone else is doing it. I'm thinking seriously of quitting, and maybe starting my own small company in a different field. Is it wrong to profit and take big bonuses when so many say it's OK?"

Pastor Davis asked, "How does Susan feel about leaving the company? You know, God gave her to you for a partner, and this decision would affect her and the children in a great way."

"She is behind me all the way. I recently realized that she felt very guilty about the situation, too," Ben replied.

"It seems like the answer you might be seeking is found in Exodus 29. Let me read a couple of verses." Pastor opened his Bible.

Exodus 23:2 Thou shalt not follow a multitude to do evil; neither shalt thou speak in a cause to decline after many to wrest judgment.
Exodus 23:8 And thou shalt take no gift: for the gift blindeth the wise, and perverteth the words of the righteous.

"I'm not using this verse to say what they are doing is illegal, but if it feels wrong to you, then I think God is trying to tell you something. If it seems unfair to you, it probably is. Large gifts tend to make people accept unfair practices and close their eyes to them. It can be kind of like an unspoken bribe just to look the other way."

"That's exactly it," answered Ben. "I'm so glad you've made it clear to me."

"Ben, I must remind you that when you turn away from anything that you feel is not right, you will have to fight hard in the battle that is sure to come. Remember what it says in Ephesians 6."

Ephesians 6:11 Put on the whole armour of God, that ye may be able to stand against the wiles of the devil.

"I suggest," the pastor went on, "that you and Susan study ***Ephesians 6: 11-18*** very intensely and spend a great deal of time in prayer in the coming days."

If We Had Known

"Oh, Abby, I am so sorry. If I had just known that the interest rates could possibly have gone this high, I would have never insisted that we buy this expensive house and all the expensive furniture, not to mention the travel and all the other things. We've been living way beyond our means.

"Now this….," Nick crumpled the foreclosure notice in his hand. "First it was my job ending after twenty years, and then you had to quit working after the car wreck, and then the unexpected repair bills."

"So many people have promised me work. I've counted on that, but it's never come about. The mortgage company said they would try and work with us, but they didn't mean it. Now we won't even have a home after the end of the month. I don't know where we'll go, Abby. I don't know what we'll do, and I certainly don't know how to tell the children."

Abby patted his shoulder with tears streaming, "I don't know what to do either, Honey. It's been one thing after the other for three years now. I think we've tried every possible thing we could do to keep this house. We both stay so depressed, and can't get by without those anxiety pills."

When the doorbell rang, Abby glanced out the front window. "It's Joel, your brother. Remember, he was supposed to stop by this afternoon."

"I guess we might as well tell him," said Nick as he opened the door. "Hi, Joel, I'm glad you're here. We need to talk to someone."

After Nick filled him in, Joel shook his head, "Wow, it seems you've just been hit with the knockout punch. You know, any fighter will tell you they usually don't see that knockout punch coming. If they had, they would have prepared.

"Satan works the same way, promising us anything, and we're deceived into believing it until the knockout punch comes. I think you would have done things differently, maybe sold the house, or even moved to another area, if you had known this was coming.

"You mentioned depression. I didn't realize it was that bad. That's Satan's number one weapon, attacking our minds and our thoughts with mental oppression that often relates to the situation we're in. It's time both of you begin to fight back!"

2 Timothy 2:4 *No man that warreth entangleth himself with the affairs of this life; that he may please him who hath chosen him to be a soldier.*

Joel went on, "Yes, you may lose this house, but you're not alone in this fight unless you want to be. Look at your picture on the wall of Jesus knocking at the door. Do you notice that the door doesn't have a door knob? There is a reason for that. The door can only be opened from the inside, to let Jesus in to help you. You have to open the door and call on Him. So far, you've tried to handle this all by yourselves.

"It's when we don't recognize that the battle is spiritual, and Satan is trying to destroy us, that he works the hardest to do just that. You both know Jesus. You need to let Him in, call on Him to help, and put everything into His hands."

"Joel, you are so right. No home is worth losing our mental abilities, and most of all our salvation over. It's time we did turn everything over to Christ and follow Him first, regardless of any house or problems we have. I know He will help us," Nick said determinedly.

Nick and Abby did lose their house. They knew it was way above what they really needed anyway. They've rented a smaller house, closer to the children's school.

A Christian brother in the church offered Nick a job in a different field, one that he had never even considered before. It's working out very well.

Two very important things happened in all of this. The first was that Nick and Abby learned to recognize spiritual battles and learned how to fight with spiritual weapons.

The next was that they learned to stay very close to Christ. They recognized that the most important things are not houses, cars and other worldly things. Faith, righteousness, holiness, and keeping a close relationship with Christ are the most important things of all.

Colossians 3:1-3 If ye then be risen with Christ, seek those things which are above, where Christ sitteth on the right hand of God.

Set your affection on things above, not on things on the earth.

For ye are dead, and your life is hid with Christ in God.

Chaos

"What happened to the patient in room two? He couldn't have walked out. He couldn't walk, period." Janice searched the ER frantically, "His wife and daughter are gone, too."

"Excuse me Miss, my wife is gone. She was in that room, and she just disappeared. Where did you take her?"

Soon the ambulances were backed up at the receiving door. There were just not enough paramedics or nurses to handle the intake. Sirens, noise, and shouting filled the air from the large city outside of the hospital. The hallways were filling with all the injured and dying. It was complete confusion and chaos. "What happened?" was the panicked cry of so many.

"Where is Dr. Bryson? Dr. Miller is gone, too. And at least a third of the nurses have disappeared." Misty turned to Karen in a confused daze. "We've got to have more help. What happened anyway? Is it some kind of terrorist attack, an earthquake?"

"No, I know what it is," Karen answered with tears streaming down her face.

"Well? What? Tell me what could cause all this confusion and terror." They were working together to stop the bleeding from the wounds of the man on the gurney in front of them. The only doctor in sight ordered them to go ahead and help the patients as best they could, since all the other doctors were backed up with desperate patients.

Karen hesitantly tried to explain. "I think it is called the Rapture. I learned about it in church before I met Jim and got caught up in this wild lifestyle. Now he won't marry me, and since I didn't want to be alone, I just moved in with him.

I've never repented of my lifestyle, even though I know it is wrong. You see, the Bible said it would occur very suddenly, and everyone should stay ready to be caught up with the other Christians when Jesus would carry them to Heaven."

"Look in my pocket, nurse." the man on the gurney gasped through his pain.

Misty pulled out a small New Testament from his pocket. "Yes, it was in I Thessalonians 4, I think, as well as I Corinthians 15, if I remember right."

"That's right," said the backslidden preacher. "I knew I was wrong, and I knew if I didn't stop, I wouldn't make the Rapture, but I never gave up sinning and I never gave up my church. I just kept on preaching and kept on sinning. I wonder if anyone in my church made it into Heaven. The pornography, I didn't want to fight it. God gave me the weapons and I ignored them." His voice was fading but he grasped both of the nurse's hands.

"You can still make it!! It will be harder now, but don't give in to Satan. Turn to God!" With his dying breath, the preacher said, "Oh God, forgive me. I'm so sorry."

Stunned, Misty and Karen went into the closest empty room. Misty turned to *I Thessalonians 4: 16-17*.

For the Lord himself shall descend from heaven with a shout, with the voice of the archangel, and with the trump of God: and the dead in Christ shall rise first:
Then we which are alive and remain shall be caught up together with them in the clouds, to meet the Lord in the air: and so shall we ever be with the Lord.

She then turned to *I Corinthians 15:51-53*.

Behold, I shew you a mystery; We shall not all sleep, but we shall all be changed,

In a moment, in the twinkling of an eye, at the last trump: for the trumpet shall sound, and the dead shall be raised incorruptible, and we shall be changed.
For this corruptible must put on incorruption, and this mortal must put on immortality

"Well I just don't believe that stuff, Misty. It's got to be a strange coincidence or something. My mama always tells me the Bible is true, but I sure don't want to give up my good times and start going to church all the time. She is always praying and reading her Bible. I just don't want to believe it."

"It's true, Karen, I know it's true. Why don't you try and call your mama. You know she would be home this time of night, if she didn't go in the Rapture."

Karen quickly dialed the number, desperately waiting for an answer to the call. "Oh, Mama, oh, no, Mama, please don't be gone." Of course, there was no answer.

In the coming days, as the truth set in, both Karen and Misty determined to repent and live a Christian life in that antichrist world. They knew what the result would be, and that before the tribulation time period ended, they would both give their lives for the cause of Christ.

Crybaby

Judy turned to Louise and Walt with tears of frustration. "I know the Word says we should never fear. I'm aware of what we are supposed to do, but I just can't conquer the fears that overwhelm me. What will happen in the future, my medical problems, my financial state? I even worry about things that are completely unfounded, things that could possibly happen. They torment me all the time."

They sat on Walt and Louise's large screened porch that overlooked the pasture land on their Texas farm. A storm began to move in from the south, with dark clouds and an occasional sound of thunder. They never tired of watching the large herd of cattle as they grazed. There were always lots of calves playing, and often there was an occasional deer at the edge of the woods.

Walt's sister, Judy, was visiting from Oregon. She remained single, although quite popular in years past; she had never committed herself to a relationship with anyone. Now she was facing numerous problems, and they could see she simply could not handle the challenges.

Walt turned and looked towards the west. "Judy, I want you to watch for the bull to come. He likes to socialize with the neighbors. That's why my fences are always in need of repair. Fences don't pose much of a problem when a two-thousand-pound bull wants to go visiting."

The storm was moving a little closer and getting louder. "He should be coming soon," remarked Louise.

"Is that him?" asked Judy. They could see a large bull running at top speed towards the corral. The thunder and lightning increased. Then they heard an unbelievable, constant bawling coming from this huge beast. It got louder as he came closer.

"Oh yes," Louise answered, laughing, "that's him, all right. His name is 'Crybaby'. You can see and hear why. In almost every way he's a full-grown fearless bull, except he is terribly afraid of thunderstorms, and always comes running home crying whenever one approaches. Our neighbors actually named him, and he's kind of the laughingstock of all the ranches around."

Walt looked at Judy, "Judy, we all have worries, fears, and anxieties. This life truly is a battlefield. There are two important things to remember. How do we face our fears, and who do we cry out to? Crybaby runs home crying. He knows there is shelter here, and the rest of the herd.

The spiritual battles we face are devastating, they tear us down by placing terrible 'what if' thoughts in our minds. We face them head-on with our heads up, knowing we are never alone in any battle. The Christian has a major resource and advantage over others who don't know where to turn.

If we run, we must run to God's Word because therein lies the help and strength we need."

Matthew 11:28-30 Come unto me, all ye that labour and are heavy laden, and I will give you rest.
Take my yoke upon you, and learn of me; for I am meek and lowly in heart: and ye shall find rest unto your souls.
For my yoke is easy, and my burden is light.

Chapter Three

The Whole Armour

Ephesians 6:11 Put on the whole armour of God, that ye may be able to stand against the wiles of the devil.
Ephesians 6:13 Wherefore take unto you the whole armour of God, that ye may be able to withstand in the evil day, and having done all, to stand.

    Paul wrote Ephesians when he was in prison in Rome. He observed Roman soldiers firsthand. He might have even been chained to one. It was very common for a prisoner to be chained to a soldier. *Acts 28:16, 20.* Being that close, Paul must have closely observed the soldier's dress and armor. The correlation of armor being necessary for Christians would have been very clearly seen.

    Christians are also soldiers, not in the Roman army, but in the army of Christ. A Roman soldier was very formidable in full armor. Christians are also formidable when dressed in the full armor provided for us.

    Verse 11 speaks of the armor being *"put on."* The armor must be in our possession and on our bodies. It cannot be thrown in the closet, left in the car, or tossed on the end table.

    God's Word doesn't say that it would automatically be put on us. It didn't say we only needed one part. It said put the whole armor on, and to put it on ourselves. Not just some of the armor, but all of it.

    Putting on the armor is a command, and not a choice. We can't say 'Father, I think I'll just sit this one out.' If we don't put the armor on and fight, we will not withstand the devil's wiles.

Armor is designed to turn aside the blows of the enemy. How important that is! If the strikes do not penetrate our spiritual covering, wounds and scars will not result. There won't be any sitting around nursing hurt feelings or worrying about 'what ifs'. Unscathed, we can keep our minds intact and concentrated on Christ.

The armor is a complete outfit, two-fold, offensive and defensive. The soldier must be fully covered and protected.

Verse 11 also tells us that putting on the armor will enable us to stand. Standing is a fighting posture. It means not cowering or turning away under pressure. Standing also means winning and overcoming, as well as conquering. The one who loses is not standing upright, but down in defeat. Only when you stand firmly, not giving in, can you overcome.

Job 19:25 For I know that my redeemer liveth, and that he shall stand at the latter day upon the earth:

This scripture points us to Jesus, the conquering redeemer, completely victorious in overcoming sin. It tells us that Jesus will STAND as the victor, the winner of the battle at the latter day.

Paul mentioned standing in verse *11, 13*, and again in verse *14* of ***Ephesians 6***. Standing means never turning your back to the enemy or backing up. The fighting posture must be upright, not slumping, sleeping, or hiding in a corner, out of the line of fire.

Standing is resisting steadfastly, holding the line. If you are not standing properly, the enemy can advance and gain a foothold. Resisting means opposing actively, fending off, and standing firm against. ***Hebrews 12:4*** reminds us it is necessary to resist unto the blood. ***James 4:7*** says to resist and he will flee. Satan is a coward when he faces resistance.

Standing can be tiring, just as in any fight. Warriors become weary, but we cannot fall asleep spiritually just because we are tired. We must stay alert and watch. Our sleeping or (spiritually lax) time is Satan's tempting time. You could be robbed of your armor or shield while you are dozing.

If you come upon a snake in the yard, you won't feel sleepy! You'll be alert. What shall I do? What kind is he? How do I deal with this?

Yet, we sleep! Sometimes we doze right through attacks and temptations, giving in and not fighting at all! *Matthew 26:41* says to watch. You will frustrate the enemy if you are alert and not spiritually groggy and drowsy.

Watch constantly! Don't relegate your spiritual time to a quick ten-minute early morning prayer and a couple of verses read. Be constant and consistent. No matter how busy, prayer can always be part of your activities. Read the Word and study every chance you get. Whatever your weaknesses, guard them very carefully. It could be your mind, your emotions, your body, your temper, or whatever your personal downfalls might be.

Our spiritual lives must be protected in all areas because the enemy attacks in many areas, not just in one. In verse 13, the word 'withstand' is used along with 'stand'. To withstand means to fight back forcefully, to oppose and to endure. It speaks of an immovable steadfastness when attacked by the enemy

We must not be lackadaisical and fight halfway. An **active** prayer life is mandatory. The Bible must always be within easy reach. There is spiritual strength in pulpit messages and fellowship with other Christians.

An evil day is any day when we are vulnerable to attack, which is every day. The attack could come in the form of a loss, a death, a conflict, or a setback of any kind. Evil days are those in which we live and contend in the battles that we presently fight. Standing and fighting in full armor must be a way of living. Knowing that Christ is with us should alleviate any fear we might have. It always helps us to remember that there is permanent victory at the end of the final battle.

At the end of ***verse 13***, Paul speaks of 'having done all, to stand'. This reminds us that we will fight to the end of this life. 'All' means doing everything we can to stand. It is being thorough in the way we fight. If you break that word, thorough, in half it says 'tho' 'rough'. Maybe the spelling isn't accurate, but the meaning is clear. Sometimes it <u>is</u> rough to do everything we can do.

Persevering in prayer and Bible study, even when other things demand our time, is not always an enjoyable task. Standing and fighting can be hard when we would like to rest or take a leave of absence. But it is necessary to finish completely, even though the road is rough.

Don't look for the glory in the fight. Forget the 'sum laude' and just look for the approval of our heavenly Father. Stay in the trenches when they are full of mud and filth. Don't give up and back down just because the battle is difficult. Christ never tells you to retreat, surrender, or give up. He doesn't say put the weapons down and stop fighting. He says onward, forward, fight on. Finish and complete the battle until He calls you home.

By accepting Christ, we enlist in His army as foot soldiers for the duration. We are always following, always fighting, continually denying self and staying in the battle.

What if you win a victory? We will win victories, but we must never be careless and let victories cause us to be unprepared for the next battle.

Surrendering All

Dawn could not take any more. Now her husband was being so short-tempered with the children in the few days he spent at home. She confronted him with his infidelity. She had known for some time, but she did not want to face it.

Her marriage vows were important to her, but in the last year, he had become impossible to live with. All of her plans of having the perfect life with her husband and children were coming apart.

Richard was rarely at home, volunteering for one overseas tour after another, all to the same little country. When she brought it all out into the open, she felt his relief. He admitted the truth and said his girlfriend was expecting a child in a few months.

Dawn knew the marriage was over, and volunteered to get out of his life. He helped her pack and move to a different city. Since he wanted to keep his newer car, he bought her an older clunker to drive, and gave her all the furniture.

Dawn helplessly looked toward the future, with no job and little experience. Now she had three children to support, knowing he wouldn't have much left over to send to help them.

In her desperation, she turned to a God that she really didn't know and begged Him to help. But instead of turning everything over to him, she continued to rely on her own abilities. She was a hard worker, and knew she would manage this challenge some way.

When a low-paying job was secured, she enrolled the two older children in school, and the little one in a nursery. She scraped by every month, managing to pay the bills and provide their needs. The family was happier to be away from the stress Richard had brought, but there was a gnawing unhappiness in Dawn's life, along with the pressure of providing for her family.

Months later, after a couple of promotions due to her hard work, the pressure eased somewhat. Dawn slowly found herself drawn to an older man who was completely her opposite. He was a strong Christian who was also divorced because of his wife's infidelity. He was a single dad raising his children. Dawn felt he would never be unfaithful to her. They married and blended their two families.

There was still something missing in Dawn's life. They attended church, but Dawn never realized she still held onto all the control in her life.

A couple of years later, her husband had a severe heart attack and there was a chance he would not recover. Dawn finally realized just how helpless she was.

There was absolutely nothing she could do to make him recover. Desperately, on her knees, she sought God and relinquished complete control. She promised to trust Him regardless of what might happen. Dawn recognized that He could handle everything when she could not. When God is in control we always have Him to rely on instead of our own inadequacies.

Ephesians 2:8,9 For by grace are ye saved through faith; and that not of yourselves: it is the gift of God:
Not of works, lest any man should boast.

Titus 3:5 Not by works of righteousness which we have done, but according to his mercy he saved us, by the washing of regeneration, and renewing of the Holy Ghost;

When Dawn finally relinquished her hold on her life and relied completely on God, she felt the unbelievable joy of finally wearing all of the armor available to a Christian.

Now all of God's protection, guiding, and leading directed her life. She knew she was in God's hands, and that He had a plan for her life. Not her plan, but His.

Her husband recovered, and they spent many happy years together, with God at the head of their marriage.

The Armour of the Word

Holly's eyes rested for a moment on her computer desktop. With a completely black background, the open Bible was quite arresting. The few shortcut icons were situated at the edge, out of the way. Because the screen was large, the verses from ***Ephesians 5:24*** through ***Philippians 1:27*** were all visible and easy to read. It was comforting to her to see the open Bible every time she turned the computer on.

She wasn't sure why she had been so impressed to put the picture of the Bible on her desktop. The scriptures on the page were the ones in ***Ephesians 6,*** about the weapons of warfare. She had been studying these for some time. These highlighted scriptures in this large, open Bible might wind up to be the cover for the book she was writing.

Now it was time to quit procrastinating and go ahead and call the technical help she needed to work out the problem on the computer. Oh, how she dreaded making the call. Often the 'help' took hours, and sometimes the problem wasn't even fixed.

A short time later, she was connected. The female voice with the Mid-Eastern accent asked if she could take control of the computer to find the problem. Holly agreed; it was much easier than trying to follow all the instructions.

When the connection was complete, there was a long pause. Finally the voice quietly asked, "Is that a Bi...ble?" Holly prayed as she answered, knowing God was working. She said softly, "Yes, it is."

"I've never seen an open Bible before!" The voice responded.

A longer pause, and then from India, reading slowly, ***"Children, obey your parents in the Lord: for this is right."***

Holly hesitated a moment and said, "That's good advice, isn't it?"

"Yes, it is," she answered.

There were more long pauses, and Holly kept silent, knowing that this lady who had never seen an open Bible was reading those two pages. Did she read about how Christ gave Himself for the church, or how we are members of His flesh? Perhaps the instructions to husbands, or workers, or did she glean knowledge about the weapons of the believer and praying?

We will never know what this lady received from God's Word that day, but we do know that the Word is anointed, and it draws people to read it.

Holly knew on that day that God had used the open Bible on the computer screen to speak to a woman from India who had never seen an open Bible.

Ever since that time, when Holly has needed technical help, the worker has immediately blacked out the desktop as they take control. She'll never know the details of what happened that day, but God does, and that's what matters.

Stand

Pastor Evans stepped to the podium as the choir finished their last song. "If everyone will please turn to *1 Corinthians 8:2*. We will start with that scripture today."

And if any man think that he knoweth any thing, he knoweth nothing yet as he ought to know.

Nate stared at the Pastor, but his mind was several miles away at the hospital with his wife, Jill.

He knew he would soon be expected to make a decision about disconnecting the life support. Nate was tormented. The family disagreed on any plan of action, and was torn apart. There had been several loud disputes. It was a terrible time. For weeks, ever since the accident, she had been in a coma, and the outcome was completely unknown.

Even the medical staff disagreed about her treatment. Nate was drained, fighting constantly to obtain the best care for her.

Since it happened, he had prayed, fasted, stayed in the Word, and sought God constantly. Jill was at a superior medical facility with the best doctors.

Being in a medical field himself, he was able to research and try to make sure that everything had been done. He even consulted with other medical experts, and traveled to other cities to make sure there was nothing else they would recommend that could be done.

This morning was the first time he had been in the church for a service, instead of at Jill's bedside. Maybe there was something else God would show him that would give him direction.

Pastor spoke of how we can think we know everything about a situation when we really don't understand the spiritual aspect at all.

Nate felt Pastor Evans was speaking directly to him. It was how he always felt when God was about to reveal a truth from a message that would be just exactly what he needed at the time. He gripped the seat of the pew and leaned forward.

"Sometimes when we have fought a certain battle for a length of time, and the battle just seems to get more intense despite all of our efforts, we need to relinquish our hold on the situation and let God take over," Pastor went on.

"There are times we fight and times when we stand, like Daniel did in the lion's den. *Ephesians 6:13, 14* tells us when we've done all we can, then to stand. Never quit praying and seeking God, but quit trying to maneuver and find a solution on your own.

"At the Red Sea, Moses told the complaining Israelites to stand still, keep quiet, and the Lord would fight for them, and *Exodus 14* tells us that He did just that."

Nate's concentration was riveted on the message. Yes, he had been in complete control, now it was time to step back and let God handle it completely.

"Let's end with *2 Chronicles 20.* In verse *17* it says:

Ye shall not need to fight in this battle: set yourselves, stand ye still, and see the salvation of the LORD with you, O Judah and Jerusalem: fear not, nor be dismayed; tomorrow go out against them: for the LORD will be with you."

"Jahaziel spoke this prophecy to the Israelites and then in verses 20-22 it tells of how Jehoshaphat, obeying God, sent out the choir to sing, and the Moabites and Ammonites were ambushed by those waiting. God can use a choir to lead the army to victory." Pastor went on, "Let go of the situation. You've done all you can do. Let God handle it in His way as only He can."

Nate arose from the altar, a complete peace flooding his being. He headed for his car, checking his cell phone on the way. Even the message from Regions Medical Center could not disturb the peace. He didn't answer the call, but drove directly to the hospital, which was only a few blocks away.

"Oh, Nate, I just tried to call you," the nurse said with tears in her eyes, "Just go on in."

The doctor stood at the bedside with a look of disbelief on his face. Jill's eyes were **open** for the first time in weeks. Recognition showed in her eyes as she saw Nate enter. He grasped her hand as the tears poured down his face, thanking God for what He had done.

Recovery was slow, but God directed it all, and through all the weeks some of God's purposes became clear to them. Nick learned a very valuable lesson about when to fight and when to stand.

Provoked

"Oh, I'm still steaming at that miserable Ruthie. She did it again, Erin. She took credit for getting that large report complete when I did all the work."

"She actually told me she did it on purpose so I wouldn't get the next promotion. She is planning to get it herself. She could see how angry I was, and she just laughed at me!" Jessie gripped the arms of her chair in the break room.

"I don't see how you can remain so calm. It will hurt you, too, if she gets the promotion." Jessie kept on angrily speaking.

Erin thought a minute before answering. "I used to let people like that bother me, but not anymore, Jessie. I was so upset one time, I actually slapped someone."

"Well, what happened? How did you conquer that terrible anger? I really need to know, Erin. The world is full of people like that, and I've got to learn how to handle the situations." Jessie leaned forward to hear what Erin would say.

"Jessie, you're a solid, mature Christian, and you represent Christ beautifully except when you are angry. You just cannot let people provoke you."

"When I had that problem, God led me to study **Ephesians 6:11** and *13*, but first He took me to **Numbers 20:8-11.**"

Numbers 20:8 Take the rod, and gather thou the assembly together, thou, and Aaron thy brother, and speak ye unto the rock before their eyes;...
Numbers 20:10.... And Moses and Aaron gathered the congregation together before the rock, and he said unto them, Hear now, ye rebels; must we fetch you water out of this rock?

Numbers 20:11 And Moses lifted up his hand, and with his rod he smote the rock twice: and the water came out abundantly…..

"This is a story with a lesson for all of us, Jessie. Moses did everything he could to bring those rebellious people into the Promised Land. Then, in a moment of anger, he showed the anger by hitting the rock instead of speaking to it. He never got to enter into that land because of this."

"You see, Satan is after the mature Christian, most of all. He loves to see someone solid in the faith fall by the wayside because of their weakness. He knows where their weak point is, and he uses whatever tool he can, which includes people who provoke us to anger."

"When we give in to anger, God is upset with us, not with that person who provoked us. We are the ones that can fall and cause others to fall." Erin went on.

"***Ephesians 6:11 and 13*** tells us we can stand against provoking and tormenting if we have on all of the armor. That full armor will be visible to others by our actions. The armor must be **put** on. It takes a conscious effort. It's something we are commanded to do, not just if we want to.

"The armor will deflect the enemy's blows, and if they don't hit us, there are no wounds or scars to heal up. It will keep our minds on Christ and enable us to stand, if it is put on.

"People used by the enemy want us to give in to anger. That's exactly what they want to see.

"You've got to understand, Jessie. Satan is very cowardly, and he will run if faced with opposition. Instead of anger, we're to resist steadfastly and hold the line calmly. We must guard our weaknesses, such as temper, carefully."

"Yes, Erin, you're exactly right. But just what did you do to keep that armor on when confronted?"

"For me, Jessie, it was real simple. I realized I had been slacking off on Bible reading, using the excuse of having to hurry to get ready in the mornings. I intentionally set the alarm 20 minutes earlier, and I made sure I spent that time reading and studying God's Word.

"I also keep a scripture CD in the car to listen to on the way to work. You can't neglect praying, either. Just doing these things made me so much more confident in those bad situations. I truly was able to stand, feeling secure about my armor being in place."

"Thank you, Erin, it makes so much sense and I certainly don't want to lose out with God."

Contending

Whitney threw her disposable gloves, mask, and gown into the contamination container and walked down the hall, stopping at the nurses' station, "I've never felt so helpless. No matter what we do, more and more become infected."

"I know," answered Edward. "These people are having enough problems healing from their surgeries here in the SICU without MRSA (Methicillin-resistant Staphylococcus aureus) infections."

Nita, who was the student nurse assigned to their wing, nodded. "It seems like every day one or two more test results come in positive, and they have to start on that special antibiotic to counteract it. I wish we could just stop it from spreading! That's the big problem. All the precautions just don't seem to be enough."

Edward responded. "These people are really suffering. The MRSA overwhelms the patients' immune system. More and more need surgery to drain the sites. It's not allowing them to heal from their original surgeries. Some are even dying from the infection."

"We just have to watch them very carefully for those original signs, such as low-grade fever or lethargy." Whitney noted. "It is so tiring on those of us that work on this wing. I am so exhausted; I can hardly hold my head up."

Edward agreed and said, "I don't know about you, but I've learned that many situations like this are spiritual. I know and believe personally that God can help us fight this if we seriously contend with spiritual weapons."

"Count me in, Edward, I agree with you." Nita answered hopefully.

"Well, not me," answered Whitney, "You know I only believe in scientific explanations and answers. I don't have time to fool with religious stuff. Nobody believes that anymore. What is the matter with you two? Just ask Doctor Peters, it's a waste of time to fool with things like that."

Dr. Peters did agree totally with Whitney, and advised the two not to bother with spiritual things. He said to just take care of themselves and try not to pick up the infection themselves, or spread it.

Edward and Nita were both Christians. They agreed to meet after work and talk about further pursuing this plan of action.

They ordered coffee at the small café and Edward began by sharing some scripture from the book of Jude.

Jude 1:3 Beloved, when I gave all diligence to write unto you of the common salvation, it was needful for me to write unto you, and exhort you that ye should earnestly contend for the faith which was once delivered unto the saints.

"Do you see, Nita, how it says *'earnestly contend.'* Remember, Jude is placed just before the book of Revelation, which takes place in the end-time. I believe with all the terrible things that are happening, it shows us just how close we are to the Rapture and the end of time."

"Contend means to put on the whole armor of God and fight with everything God provides for us. Contend is not a passive word. It is forceful, and it means to compete against a contrary doctrine. It's the doctrine of the world view that tells us we are wrong and don't need to fight this."

Edward continued. "If we rely on self-preservation the way Dr. Peters said, it will defeat us. We have to fight positively with faith. Faith and doubt don't even exist together. We must contend against anything that competes against the knowledge of God. We cannot let the secular opinions of others influence our fight."

Jeremiah 12:5 If thou hast run with the footmen, and they have wearied thee, then how canst thou contend with horses? And if in the land of peace, wherein thou trustedst, they wearied thee, then how wilt thou do in the swelling of Jordan?

"That is so true, Edward, if we back down and retreat, it's only a short-term peace. But if we continue to earnestly contend, we will have the victory. Remember, there will be others fighting with us. The families of those patients, many of them are Christians.

"'If' or 'what if' cannot be allowed in our minds or our speech in the battle. We will replace that with 'what is' and 'what will be.'"

Edward and Nita seriously began to 'contend'. They prayed, fasted, encouraged each other, and bound together with other believers in this battle.

The very day they began to fight, there was a turnaround in the Surgical Intensive Care Unit. It was the first day in several weeks that there were no new MRSA cases. As they continued to fight, giving up rest and sleep to fight and contend earnestly, healing came to the floor. Within a few days all the patients began to heal and look and feel better.

You never fight alone when you 'earnestly contend'. God is right there beside you.

Chapter Four

Loins Girt About With Truth

Paul writes of the armor in the order it would be put on.

Ephesians 6:14a Stand therefore, having your loins girt about with truth,

The girdle was not exactly part of the armor, but it was extremely necessary to bind the garments together underneath, in order that the armor could be worn. The clothing was traditionally long and flowing. Before a race could be run or a battle fought, the garments had to be bound or girded. The belt gathered in the tunic and helped to steady the breastplate. If the buckle was not firm, the clothing would slip out and trip the soldier.

The wide belt held the scabbard in which the sword was sheathed. It had loops for the ropes and other tools. It also held the rations bag. This could be emptied to hold the spoils of gold and silver won in combat. The belt also held the darts necessary for the battle. If the belt was not properly fastened, it would cost the soldier his life.

Daily the soldier put on the girdle to hold the armor in place. It wrapped around his vital area, just as we must have the Word wrapped around us daily.

It is so necessary that we hold firm to all of the teachings in the Word. The culture we live in is constantly trying to encroach, infiltrate, and change the Word of God. The Word is the standard for truth.

The Bible speaks of girding as a preparatory action, a pulling together in preparation for something.

1 Peter 1:13 Wherefore gird up the loins of your mind, be sober, and hope to the end for the grace that is to be brought unto you at the revelation of Jesus Christ;

     There is only one 'truth'; it is based upon the Word of God. Truth involves both sincerity in our hearts and the knowledge of the Word. The loins are the spirit and mind that 'wear' the truth.

     The actions of our mind and spirit can be strong or weak. Therefore we have strong mature Christians, as well as immature, weak ones.

     If you seek after understanding of the truth, and hold fast, and base your life on this clear understanding, you should grow into a strong, mature Christian.

     Satan always has sinister plans to rob the Christian of the truth of the doctrine. His plan can come in the form of false teachers, misleading literature, and other erroneous materials that we are exposed to.

     The only defense is to be girded (upheld or wrapped) in the truth, and pray for the knowledge and understanding of the Word to be clear in our minds.

     Remember the Bereans who searched the scripture daily to verify the doctrine that Paul was preaching. ***Acts 17:11***. They refused to believe until it was proven by God's Word. Many believed after they confirmed the Word.

     Satan's tactics are deplorable. He wouldn't say, "Oh, those teachings are completely wrong." We would know better. Instead, he would cause conflict and plant seeds of doubt in your minds. He would also make his 'new' teaching look completely irresistible. It would sound so good we could be deceived if we did not know the word of truth.

     Many are completely misled by following what 'sounds good.' They are ignorant of the truth, and they accept it when they hear that if they just believe 'something', they will be OK. They believe there are many ways to Heaven, but the truth plainly states that there are many roads to hell, but only one road to Heaven, which is Jesus Christ.

It is so important that we know and strengthen our knowledge of the truth, because the evil forces are strong enough to destroy faith. Some are even turned into 'searchers', those that constantly search for learning, but never really come into the knowledge of the truth.
2 Timothy 3:7.

Some are content with the 'milk' of the Word, as new babies, *1 Peter 2:2,* but never move on to the 'meat,' *John 4:32,* that is able to sustain the believer against the constant opposition.

The doctrine of the truth is what will ground and establish the Christian. ***Ephesians 4*** tells us we are no longer children to be tossed to and fro. In ***Nehemiah 8,*** we are shown how the priests reading the law caused the Israelites to comprehend and understand the law.

God gave us pastors, teachers, and other leaders to bring us the messages of His Word. We must pay attention and learn the doctrine of the truth. This doesn't take the place of our own searching the Scripture, but it will enhance and help us to grow.

The truth of God is liberating. Only those who completely cling to it are free, *John 8:32*. Satan's slaves are in complete bondage to a very hard taskmaster.

Because truth involves the sincerity of our hearts, we must keep our hearts and guard them with strict discipline. Have you ever walked across a room and tripped, yet when you looked there was nothing there to trip on? It was a perfectly flat, smooth floor. The shoestrings are tied. Did you drag your foot just a tiny bit? Did the shoe stick to the floor for a second? This is just what your heart can do. It can stumble when you don't even see a problem.

That's why ***Proverbs 4:23*** says: ***Keep thy heart with all diligence; for out of it are the issues of life.***

Jeremiah also speaks of the heart being deceitful and desperately wicked, ***Jeremiah 17:9.***

It's wonderful that we can pray that God will search our hearts for evil ways daily to keep the heart in check. Jeremiah says that the Lord does search the heart, and He knows us much better than we know ourselves.

The belt or girdle not only held the weapons of the warfare, but it gave strength and support to the wearer's loins. The loins usually refer to the lower back, or the hips and lower abdomen, a region of strength in the body. When this area is girded up, it is preparing to do something involving support or strength.

Psalms 18:39a speaks of the one who strengthens us. ***For thou hast girded me with strength unto the battle***:

Isaiah 11: 5 speaks of undergirding the truth and supporting the integrity in the inward parts.

And righteousness shall be the girdle of his loins, and faithfulness the girdle of his reins.

Carried by the Unseen Hand

Dani pondered the events of the last twenty-four hours and silently praised God as she drove across the hot, dry desert heading back home. Then she thought, yes, that is truly just like God. She had prayed for a way to represent Christ to her family at this reunion, a way that they could recognize it could only be Him. She also prayed for an opportunity to witness to her sister of God's love and protection. He answered her prayer, as always, in an unexpected way. And little did she realize that there was another miracle ahead.

She drove to the reunion with her sister because her sister just didn't want to fly with all her medical equipment. It was a long drive in the July heat. Dani did a lot of the driving because Sue had a difficult time with the heat and the altitude, and she didn't like to drive in the larger cities. Both tried to drive carefully, knowing their reflexes weren't quite as quick as they used to be.

In that large Western city, it was decided that a wheelchair would be necessary for Sue. Dani also wanted to fill up the gas tank to be ready to leave the next day. She prepared to run these errands while Sue took a nap. Their younger niece, Rita, quickly volunteered to pick up the wheelchair and get gas, since she knew the area quite well. They hesitated to take advantage of her giving up her afternoon, but in the end agreed to let her go.

When Rita pulled out of the gas station into five lanes of fairly heavy traffic and began to merge with them, the brakes completely gave out on the van. Suddenly, she had no brakes at all and was in the middle of five lanes of dense traffic.

It was a complete miracle that she steered carefully and only scraped one car before coming to a halt. Another miracle was that neither Rita nor the other driver was hurt at all. Both vehicles were dented and scraped, and Rita's needed to be towed to the brake repair shop.

If either Dani or Sue had been at the wheel, the results probably would have been far different, as their reflexes were much slower. All agreed it had to be a miracle.

The next day, after a tremendous amount of brake work, the vehicle was pronounced safe to drive, and Dani and Sue left for the long trip home. The day was fairly uneventful until just before stopping for the night; the red brake light came on.

Only one repairman in that tiny town was open on a Saturday evening. He admitted he didn't know a lot about brakes, but topped off the brake fluid and checked to make sure the brakes were working. He said that was all he could do. The brake light continued to burn.

They secured a room and made quite a few phone calls to anxious relatives, trying to glean advice. They really needed to get home the next day for many reasons and hadn't they just had the brakes completely repaired? There would be no one in that small town to even look closely at the brakes until Monday morning.

Dani called her church family to pray with her and she urgently went to the Lord in prayer that night, praying for some time that the Lord would guide them and direct them. Even though all had agreed it was a miracle no one was hurt in the first incident, Dani still had not had an opportunity to witness personally to her sister about the Lord's protecting power and saving grace.

Finally, Dani felt the Lord girding her up, peacefully comforting and quieting her spirit. She knew He would be with them and take care of the situation.

The next morning, they started the car and carefully tested the brakes several times. The brake light was not on! Sue told Dani she really wanted to go on towards home and

Dani agreed, secure in knowing God would take care of them.

They drove over 500 miles across the hot desert to reach home that evening. The brake light never again came on. The next morning, in a quiet time before Dani went on to catch her plane home, she was able to share and witness to her sister of all God had done. Sue listened quietly, recognizing His power is real. At a later time, she would ask Jesus into her heart to save and keep her personally.

Real or Counterfeit

2 Corinthians 11:13, 14 ***For such are false apostles, deceitful workers, transforming themselves into the apostles of Christ.***
And no marvel; for Satan himself is transformed into an angel of light

Eric excitedly asked his brother, "Well, didn't I tell you it was the greatest church ever? It's so interesting, and yet, there are no demands at all. Everyone is free to just come in when they want to and participate as much or as little as they feel led to. No requirements, no rules. It has none of the hellfire preaching or anything, just a lot of fun and music. It's got to be the best church around here. It really suits us."

Charles hesitated as they were getting in the car, "It really didn't seem much like a church."

"I know! That's why it's so great. None of that worry about needing to go to the altar, or repenting, or anything. There's no fear that if you don't go to the altar and repent, you won't make it to Heaven."

"That's called conviction, Eric. If people aren't convicted of their sin, they won't get saved. I think your church is a good social club where people can go and get together, but it won't do anything about drawing them closer to God or giving them the joy and peace that salvation brings. Yes, it's the repenting of sin and asking Jesus into your heart that gives us eternal hope of heaven when we leave this world."

"Charles, I think I knew what you were going to say," Eric responded. "But just tell me how you immediately knew? I was so sure it was a great church. How do you tell?"

"Eric, you know part of my work at the bank is training new tellers. How do you think we train the tellers to tell real money from counterfeit?"

"Well," Eric said thoughtfully, "I guess you show them all the fake money you can to get them familiar with that stuff."

"No, that's not what we do at all. The tellers are taught what the genuine is, not what the fake is. They must know the real money by the touch, the look, the weight, the sound, the color. Everything about the real they have to know. Then it's very easy to discern when money is not right and they are handed something fake.

"Eric, that's exactly why we attend church often, and why we read and study God's Word. It's why we go to Sunday school. In this time of massive deceptions, we have to know everything about what we believe and why we believe it.

"In God's true church, He reigns as the head. Everything that is said and done, from the music to the preaching, should glorify Him. Repentance and salvation by the shed blood of Jesus Christ must be preached as the only way to Heaven. There is time for singing and fellowshipping also, but God must be the head of it all.

"Eric, when you repent of sin, and accept Christ as the Lord of your life, you will want to study and learn more. Your discernment will grow as you grow as a Christian, and you will also be able to tell the fake from the real."

John 8:31 b ... If ye continue in my word, then are ye my disciples indeed;
And ye shall know the truth, and the truth shall make you free.

The Truth Carries Us

"Marie, I don't really think I'll to be able to go on. The hurt is so real. It's an actual pain in my heart. I miss him so much and I really don't see how I can live without him." Bethany sobbed in her friend's arms.

"Yes, Honey, I know how badly it hurts. Have you been able to read the Word and let the truth of God's Word help to comfort you?" Marie asked.

"No, about all I do is cry and take those pills the doctor gave me to knock me out. I want to quit taking them, but I don't think I'm strong enough," answered Bethany.

Marie opened her Bible and said, "Bethany I know how strong a Christian Ross was, and you've always depended greatly on the Lord. Sometimes the enemy uses tragedies as a way of sidetracking our mind and keeping us from thinking straight. We've got to remember that our help comes from God, not from ourselves and how we feel, but what God's Word says." Marie began to read.

1 Corinthians 15:26   The last enemy that shall be destroyed is death.
1 Corinthians 15:19   If in this life only we have hope in Christ, we are of all men most miserable.

"Bethany, for the Christian in all the spiritual battles we fight in this life, the ultimate battle and the ultimate victory is the victory over death."

"It's the day of supreme graduation out of Satan's territory and into the presence of our loving God. The pain of loss that we feel is eased so much when we contemplate their completeness and wholeness in Christ and the life of complete peace and joy that they are living now."

"We often say, intending to comfort, that 'they are in a much better place now.' The statement is true, but we can't even comprehend the overwhelming joy that surrounds them now."

"You might not know, Bethany, that we lost a child when she was only twelve. Shortly after she died, God gave me a vision and allowed me a brief glimpse of her. She had always been sickly and was never able to run and play the way the other children did."

"In that vision, she was **running.** I can't tell you what her surroundings looked like, only the impression of overwhelming beauty. She was dressed in the purest white garment that emanated glowing rays. The joy on her face was so gloriously beautiful; a joy that we had never witnessed before in this life," she read again:

1 Corinthians 15:53 For this corruptible must put on incorruption, and this mortal must put on immortality.

"You see Bethany, she was no longer in this world of corruptions, pain, and tears. She had put on immortality. Her joyful, complete, eternal life was entirely different from this earthly life, which is full of sorrow even in the happy times."

I Corinthians 15:54b...Death is swallowed up in victory.
1 Corinthians 15:55 O death, where is thy sting? O grave, where is thy victory?

"Bethany, Ross won his final battle! He is victorious and he left this world as a conqueror. There is no cancer in Heaven. Just imagine his pain-free body. We have so much more to go to Heaven for today than we did two weeks ago."

"Oh, Marie, I feel so much better. You've reminded me that our strength comes from being girded with the truth of God's Word. The loss is painful for me, but I remember now where I have to turn, when the burden is too heavy for me."

***John 14:27** Peace I leave with you, my peace I give unto you: not as the world giveth, give I unto you. Let not your heart be troubled, neither let it be afraid*.

Overwhelmed

Sheri carried her personal things out to her car. She was very dejected. The job enabled her to get by without asking for help, and now it was gone. She was fired for telling a customer the truth.

She had enjoyed working in the Christian book store and getting a great discount on books. Some of the books they sold were just not accurate, and when people asked her opinion, she had to tell them the truth.

Some people wrote gimmicky books that would border on the truth, but actually were far from the truth of the scripture. Sheri couldn't understand why this type of book sold so well and deceived so many.

Now the enormity of her situation began to overwhelm her. There weren't a lot of jobs she could do because of her physical problems. First cancer and all the treatments for that, and recently she had been diagnosed with another really rare disease. This would make it impossible to do any type of physical labor, and many more medical bill would be piling up.

Her husband left her last year. She was horrified when he left her for another man and admitted his homosexuality to her. They had been married for twenty-nine years.

The floodwaters from a summer storm had ruined so many things in her house, and completely wiped out all her savings as she made repairs. She didn't know that her insurance company didn't cover floods.

Her daughter lived in another state and rarely contacted her. Very often Keri didn't answer the phone when Sheri called her, either. She was living in sin and running from God, even with everything she had been taught.

Her sister lived nearby, but she only wanted to argue with her about the scriptures. She had never wanted to live the Christian life as Sheri did, and thought just a perfunctory association with her formal church was all that was needed.

Sheri drove home and curled up in her favorite chair with the Bible in her lap. She prayed, letting the hot tears run down her face.

"Why, Lord? I'm not sure how much more I can handle. I know my strength is in you, but I'm getting so tired of just trying to exist in this world."

Looking down at the open Bible, she read the answer to her prayer.

Revelation 12:12 Therefore rejoice, ye heavens, and ye that dwell in them. Woe to the inhabiters of the earth and of the sea! <u>for the devil is come down unto you, having great wrath, because he knoweth that he hath but a short time.</u>

"Yes, Lord, I know that is so very accurate. I also know that with your help we will be able to continue on and face these torments."

Sheri then turned to one of her favorite scriptures - **Ephesians 6**. When she read about the loins girt about with truth, she remembered just how God's Word would carry us during these hard times.

As long as we stay in the Word with reading and study, the truth of the Word surrounds us like that belt that went around the soldier. It holds the tools and food necessary, and the darts needed for the fight. It wraps around a vital area and holds the armor in place.

We actually wear the Word in our spirit and our mind. Just like it supported the soldier and gave him strength, it will do the same for us.

Knowing God's Will

Justin walked down the hallway to the youth pastor's office. It seemed like the entire world was against him, and it was just not fair. After all, he was eighteen years old now, and had earned the right to relax a little and not have people hound him all the time.

Brother Aaron listened carefully to Justin's complaint. "Let me see if I understand, Justin. You wanted to take a year off from school before starting college, and your parents said fine, but they wanted you to find a job and do something productive."

"You didn't agree, so you've been couch-surfing with friends until their parents kicked you out. Your friends with their own places wanted you to contribute to expenses, but you wanted to spend your money on yourself, not helping with someone else's rent."

"Now you're hoping I can send you to someone in the church who will take you in. Is this correct?"

"Well, yeah, I guess so." Justin responded. "But you know I'm a good person, and I love God, and love to come to church. I'm not into anything bad, like drugs or alcohol. I even got a few jobs, but I didn't like the hours they wanted me to work, so I quit."

"Justin, what you want to do is instantly enter into the adult world with lots of fun, but no responsibilities," Brother Aaron responded. "That sounds good, but unfortunately, it's not the way it works. The Word says we earn our living by the sweat of our brow. You've been living on the goodwill of others. If you take one little letter out of that word goodwill, you would have God Will."

"Let's just look for a minute and see what God will want you to do. First of all, you have to hear God's Word to know God's will. You've missed a lot of church lately, so I'm not sure if you are listening to God at all."

"Truth has to be associated with and acted upon. It's not enough to say 'I believe,' you must walk in it. Believing is not the same as walking."

3 John 1:3-5 *For I rejoiced greatly, when the brethren came and testified of the truth that is in thee, even as thou walkest in the truth.*
I have no greater joy than to hear that my children walk in truth.

"Your thinking is a bit flawed, due to the secular way of thinking that, when one reaches the age of eighteen, they can do anything they want. We never reach the point in this Christian life that we can do anything we want."

"Our responsibilities change, but we still have to obey God, and obey those in authority over us. It can still be sinful, whether it's something illegal or not. Sinful things are things that draw us away from God and away from doing what is right."

3John 1:11 *Beloved, follow not that which is evil, but that which is good. He that doeth good is of God: but he that doeth evil hath not seen God.*

"I should have known you would just side with them, and not try and see my point at all," Justin flared. "Just never mind, I'll find someplace. I don't need you to help."

Justin marched out the door, determined to have his own way and do as he wanted. Months later he finally realized what everyone had been trying to tell him was correct, and he was the one who was wrong. He had to learn some very hard lessons first, but he matured and learned from his mistakes.

Chapter Five

Breastplate of Righteousness

Ephesians 6:14b ...and having on the breastplate of righteousness;

The breastplate of righteousness was closely related to the girdle of truth because it speaks of uprightness or moral integrity. The breastplate in Paul's time could cover just the breast, or the breast and back, or the entire body, with separate pieces for the arms and legs.

It always covered the breast and it was known as the heart-protector. Made of bronze or chain mail, it often had a back piece that covered the back. It was probably the heaviest piece of the armor and the most difficult to put on, but the protection was very necessary.

True righteousness is an attribute of God alone. It includes His spotless holiness and His perfect obedience to the law while on this earth, suffering the penalty for our sins.

Man in himself is not capable of making himself righteousness. It can only come through Christ's atoning work. When we are saved and have saving faith, His righteousness is in us.

Romans 3 and 4 tell us that the saving faith in God is imputed or counted for righteousness.

Romans 4:3, 5, 6 For what saith the scripture? Abraham believed God, and it was counted unto him for righteousness.

But to him that worketh not, but believeth on him that justifieth the ungodly, his faith is counted for righteousness.

Even as David also describeth the blessedness of the man, unto whom God imputeth righteousness without works,

According to Noah Webster in the 1872 edition of his dictionary, righteousness is equivalent to holiness. It means comprehending holy principles and conforming to divine law. Holiness is used interchangeably with righteousness in this writing.

Holiness indicates an intimate relationship with God. The Christian should live in perfect harmony and in perfect fellowship with Him, set apart from worldliness and growing in sanctification, which is a natural fruit of holiness. It means reflecting the character of God and abiding in Him.

Notice the linking word in the scripture, 'and' when speaking of the girdle of truth and the breastplate of righteousness. Truth and righteousness - holiness - are joined together, and therefore they have to go together.

It means we must bind ourselves with that pure, holy behavior. Peter exhorted Christians to be holy because God Himself is holy, *1 Peter 1:16.* Paul delivers a strong warning against not having righteousness.

Romans 1:18 *For the wrath of God is revealed from heaven against all ungodliness and unrighteousness of men, who hold the truth in unrighteousness;*

The breastplate reminds us that our protection is not from any works we might have done, but only what Christ has done in our lives. If we bind ourselves completely with that righteousness of God's will and His love, it will serve to protect from the stabs of the enemy.

Our efforts to live righteously can be difficult sometimes, just as the breastplate was difficult to put on. If we are covered with God's righteousness, the enemy has no access to attack us.

Holiness is what Satan would try to steal from all Christians. Satan doesn't mind if you are wealthy, powerful, or successful. What he covets and wants to take from you is your holiness.

One of the garments of the priesthood was a breastplate. It held precious stones engraved with the names of the ten tribes. It was not as large as the fighting breastplate Paul referred to, but it was made exactly according to God's holy pattern.

It held the Urim and the Thummim, and was called the righteous breastplate. It was to be worn over the heart of the priest when he went in before the Lord. ***Exodus 28:30***

Always covering the vital heart, the breastplate serves to protect our hearts from the painful accusations that come against us. It is protection against the things that stab a heart and cause numerous, painful heartbreaking situations in the believer. It is a strong weapon of defense against the enemy's evil tactics.

Revelation 9 speaks of demonic locusts that will torment people in the tribulation. It tells of their breastplates of iron. By covering their vulnerable chest, there will be no weapon that will be able to stop them. The breastplate of righteousness can protect and do the same for us.

A soldier without a breastplate wouldn't survive in combat. It would be so easy for the enemy to find a vital place to hit.

Sin must be constantly and consistently cleansed from our lives. Paul said that he died daily in ***I Corinthians 15:31***. Sin has an ugly way of coming back and renewing itself in our lives if not put under the blood constantly.

Never tire of repenting and asking God to search your heart for any evil way.

It's not enough to avoid sin and constantly keep it out of our lives. It's also necessary to mature in Christ and do everything we can to grow into the person we are meant to be in Him. The closer we are to Christ, the more strength we will have to live holy lives.

Righteousness Goes With You

When the supervisor announced at the meeting that Kaiden would be promoted effective immediately, there was a murmur in the room. Everyone knew he had worked very hard to earn the position.

Later that day, on their way to the break room, Jim and Kaiden entered at the same time.

"Well, congratulations, Kaiden, you've worked very hard. Thank God you received the promotion," Jim smiled as he shook Kaiden's hand.

Kaiden replied, "Well, thanks, but God surely didn't have anything to do with it. I worked really hard without any help to earn this. I'm surprised you don't resent not getting the promotion yourself. You're a hard worker, too."

"No, Kaiden, I'm really happy for you. You see, I trust God with everything that concerns me. He knows the end from the beginning. There is a reason that this promotion wasn't for me. The added responsibility might be too much right now. I'll continue to do my best at work and trust God with the future."

"But, Jim, don't you feel a lack of control when you don't plan and try to have goals toward your future?"

"Oh I have goals, Kaiden, but they have to line up with God's goals for my life and He lets me know if I get off track and too dependent on my own resources, instead of His. It's really a wonderful feeling knowing that He has all the pressure and plans under His control. I don't have to worry and strive and wonder what is ahead. Instead, I just trust Him and do what He has enabled me to do."

"Well I have to agree, it's really hard when some of my plans that I've worked so hard for don't work out, Kaiden admitted. My wife and I don't agree on a lot of things I've planned, and it's really hard to have conflict in the home."

"That's true, Kaiden. Why don't you and your family come over Saturday for a cook-out, and we can talk some more about who should have control. Perhaps we can help you and your family with some needed direction in your lives."

"That sounds great, Jim. We'll be there. I can tell you have something important in your life that I don't have."

~~~

Proverbs 3:5,6   Trust in the LORD with all thine heart; and lean not unto thine own understanding.
In all thy ways acknowledge him, and he shall direct thy paths

The righteousness or holiness of a Christian doesn't start and end at the place of worship. Indeed, it must go with him as a part of his being in the workplace, in the school, in the grocery store, on vacation and in everything he does and every place he goes. It cannot be put on the shelf when a Christian is around those who have not accepted Chist. The light of holiness must shine and extend out to those that have no hope.

Continuing On

Carolee turned the key to the outside door and entered the office. Her boss was gone to a conference, so she had the office to herself for the next two days.

Humming to herself, she thought of just how great her life was. Soon it would be her and Luke's one-year anniversary. They were so very happy together. They loved working in the church as a team, teaching the young adult class. They shared so many of the same interests, and more than anything they wanted to be in God's perfect will in everything they did.

It was a slow day at first, and then she had several people at a time to take care of. One man was a little agitated when she took his payment.

"I can't afford this miserable insurance. The rates keep going up all the time," he grumbled.

It was kind of strange; Carolee never even saw him leave the office. She usually called a greeting to each customer and a cheery 'Come back soon' when they left, but she was busy figuring a quote for someone when he must have left.

Finally 12:00 o'clock approached, and Carolee put the 'Back at One O'clock' sign in the door and locked it before she went into the little kitchen/dining room in the back.

"Oh!" She was startled to see the agitated man sitting at the little table. "What are you doing back here?" She questioned.

"Well you take enough of my money every month, I thought maybe you and I could spend a little time together," he leered as he moved towards her.

Carolee turned to run towards the side door, but he was too fast, and grabbed her, covering her mouth with his huge hand. He choked her with the intention of causing her to pass out, and to keep her from screaming, but he didn't realize his strength against the small woman, and she stopped breathing entirely.

Panicking, he dragged her body out the side door to the woods and tried to camouflage her with some dead branches and debris.

Luke looked up from his desk and was surprised to see the two deputies approach.

"Mr. Myers?" one of them asked.

"Yes," Luke replied. "What can I do for you?"

"I'm sorry to tell you this, Mr. Myers, but we have bad news about your wife." The officer told him all they knew at the time.

Luke was devastated at the news. During the next few weeks he walked in complete shock. It was difficult to sleep, eat, or work. He spent many hours in prayer and reading the Bible.

Months later, while having dinner with his friend, Peter, they discussed what had happened.

"I don't know how you made it through that situation, Luke."

"It was hard. I felt like my heart had been ripped right out of me. When I really began to study in Ephesians about the breastplate of righteousness, it helped."

*E*phesians 6:14b ...and having on the breastplate of righteousness

"The breastplate protects us from situations that hurt the heart." Luke went on.

"I developed a very intimate relationship with God. In doing so, He helped me to understand His holy principles better. It has seemed to set me apart from the world, and I hope I reflect God's character in my life. Of course, I understand it's not what we have done, but what He has done in us," Luke said thoughtfully.

"It's really amazing. You're an inspiration to the entire church. Now you're taking on that ministry of ministering to those who grieve. That's quite a task in our large church," said Peter.

"Perhaps it's where God wanted me all the time," Luke pondered. "One probably has to grieve intensely before he can minister to others that grieve."

Distractions

Kandy grabbed her backpack and ran out the back door. She had overslept again, and now she would really have to push the speed limit to make it to school on time.

If Mom and Dad didn't have to leave so early for their jobs, maybe they could double-check to make sure she was up on time.

Oh, no! As she started the car and raced out of the drive, she remembered it was Tuesday. This is the day that the Students of Faith club met before school, and she was supposed to bring the devotion. She had failed again.

It was happening so much lately. She knew if she didn't bring the history and the French grade up quickly, she would fail those two subjects, and possibly the entire senior year because of it. She didn't even get to the French review last night because Ricky and her other friends just kept calling and texting.

It was so nice to be noticed by him and then he asked her to go with him, she certainly wasn't going to refuse. She loved to talk to him, and he was taking really easy subjects this year, so the late nights didn't seem to bother him.

This afternoon she had to work at the pizza shop until it closed, so there was no chance of study until late. Tomorrow night was Friday and the date with Ricky. Saturday she had to work again. Saturday night was a great party with her friends. Kandy knew she was in over her head, but had no idea what to do about it.

She just couldn't give anything up. Everything was too important. The money from the job really helped with her wardrobe, and she had to take all these subjects to graduate in the spring. Ricky wouldn't understand if she told him they needed to break up, or at least just be friends until they graduated. He would probably start dating Monica.

Kandy squeezed through the light as it was turning red and upped the speed a little more, trying to get to the school before the final bell rang.

Then she heard the siren behind her and saw the red light flashing. "Oh, no," she moaned, "that's all I need."

Mr. Strickland shook his head as he made out the tardy slip. "I want your parents to both sign this, Kandy. This is the second time you've been late this week, and the fifth time for this semester. It's got to stop."

"Yes, sir, I'll have it back to you in the morning," Kandy said as she turned to walk out of his office.

That evening the pizza shop wasn't very busy, and Kandy asked her boss if she could leave early.

"Mom, Dad, I've got to have some help," she sighed as she entered the kitchen.

After hearing the story, most of which they were aware of, her dad asked, "What do you think is the problem, Kandy? You know the subjects aren't any harder this year than they were last year. Are you praying and asking God for His guidance before taking on more obligations? I especially don't like the speeding toschool; perhaps the bus would be best, for a while."

"Oh, Dad, there are just so many distractions during the senior year, and with my job and well…with Ricky, it doesn't seem like there is enough time to get it all done. I know God should come first before everything. I've not been praying at all, or even reading the Word."

Later, after a long conference, her parents found Kandy sitting at her desk with her Bible open. "I opened the Word to Ecclesiastes and this is the verse I found," she told them.

Ecclesiastes 11:4 He that observeth the wind shall not sow; and he that regardeth the clouds shall not reap.

Kandy went on, "I believe this is speaking to me about distractions, the things that get in the way of what is really important. I've gotten really distracted about what comes first right now. I realize I've got lots of time to work and make money in the future. There's also lots of time to devote to friends and dating, and especially talking and texting on the phone.

"Mom, Dad, I'm really sorry that I've gotten off track and let you down. If you will pray with me, I'll spend more time on the really important things. Yes, I agree, I should ride the bus for a while until you think I should drive again. Any other suggestions are welcome, too."

Her mom put her arms around her and said, "You know we'll help in every way we can as long as you do your part."

Ephesians 5:15,16 See then that ye walk circumspectly, not as fools, but as wise,
Redeeming the time, because the days are evil.

~~~

Satan loves nothing better than distracting Christians with seemingly important things. These distractions are meant to keep them so busy and involved until they completely forget what is <u>really</u> important. Our God is a God of order. It's imperative to pray often that God will lead us in an orderly way, concentrating on the things that are most important first. This serves to keep our priorities in order, and to keep Godly things first in our lives, followed by the task He has given us at the time, whether it is job, school, or service. Everything else will either fall into place or fall by the wayside as unimportant, according to the time we are in.

Setting an Example

Sam and Terri Morgan were just a few blocks from home that Sunday after church. They had guests arriving for dinner, and were hurrying to get home and put the finishing touches on the meal before friends arrived.

"Do you see that?" asked Sam, leaning on his horn. They pulled right in front of me and then stopped. Now I can't make my turn. Hey!!" Sam yelled out the window, "get out of my way."

"Now, Honey, I'm sure they'll move as soon as the traffic lets them through," Terri said, trying to calm him.

Sam opened the door and stood up. "Why did you pull in my lane anyway? Move over!"

"Ya wanna make me, mister?" jeered the young rough-looking man in the pick-up. "You all dressed up in your fancy suit."

Sam angrily tore off his coat and slammed out of the car as the children in the back seat watched anxiously and began to cry. "I'll teach that smart-alecky jerk to block me!"

At the same time, Charley Wilson, who was behind them, got out of his car. Charley lived two doors down from them.

"Sam, let's not let this go any further. The children are upset, and it's not worth fighting here on the street," Charley calmly said, catching hold of Sam's arm to distract him.

"But, did you see…" Sam was cut off by squealing tires as the red pickup pulled into the traffic. Deflated, he turned to get in his car. "You're right, Charley, I've got to learn to control my temper."

When Sam left the church that day, he left his Christian example, which is following Jesus. Righteousness must be a part of us every moment. It isn't something we pick up and put down at will, depending on the circumstances.

If Jesus is in our hearts, completely and totally, He will control upsetting circumstances that without Him could control us. This affair could have escalated into something Sam would have regretted forever. The example set in front of others, and his children, would have been difficult to repair.

When we ask Jesus to control all of our life, our emotions, our thoughts and our actions, He will provide a calming wisdom in upsetting situations.

Isaiah 58:11 a. And the LORD shall guide thee continually.........
Luke 1:79 To give light to them that sit in darkness and in the shadow of death, to guide our feet into the way of peace.

Chapter Six

Feet Shod with the Preparation of the Gospel of Peace

Ephesians 6:15 And your feet shod with the preparation of the gospel of peace;

When the breastplate had been put into place, the soldier would put on his strong boots that laced high over the ankles. These were studded thickly on the sole with carefully-placed hobnails. The nails kept a soldier from slipping, as well as helping him to maintain great speed on long marches over rough terrain. The way the boots fit and were made helped the soldier to have both protection and good mobility.

Without the trucks, airplanes and tanks of modern warfare, it was often necessary for the soldier to walk long distances. The proper shoes were very necessary. It's interesting that the Christian life often is also compared to a 'walk'. How we walk through this life makes all the difference.

Proper footwear helps every Christian to spiritually walk and stand strong, having good balance in difficult places when we are fighting battles.

The peace of the gospel enables the warrior to stand firmly in the midst of all the warring turmoil the enemy can stir up.

Isaiah 52:7 speaks of the beauty of the feet of those who bring good news. Paul wrote in Romans, referring to the scripture in Isaiah:

Romans 10:15 And how shall they preach, except they be sent? as it is written, How beautiful are the feet of them that preach the gospel of peace, and bring glad tidings of good things!

Part of a soldier's duties is to bring life-changing messages to others; messages that can determine the outcome of the battle. It is vital that the soldier be prepared to carry and deliver this message of eternal life.

The gospel carries the New Testament message of "good news." It's actually the most joyful, glorious news anyone could carry to others, the news of the Savior forgiving all of our sins, dying for us, and then rising again to live forever, so that we may have eternal life by simply accepting Him as Lord and acknowledging His sacrifice for us.

Despite the battle raging around us, we must be prepared and ready at any moment to take the gospel to others. It's necessary to have knowledge and dependence personally on the gospel to bring it to others. In the middle of that battle, we must have the message of peace ready to give out where it is needed.

The gospel message can only be shared with others if you have the joy of the Lord within yourself. It cannot be the joy that the world gives.

How does a Christian reflect that joy of knowing Christ? James speaks of joy as being merry. *James 5:13*. He said if you are merry, sing psalms. That reflects joy as praise directly back to the Father.

Why do Christians reach out for the things of happiness this world holds, instead of the things of Christ? Has the gospel message become stale, old, and no longer joyful? Oh, no! It's still the same and will always be the same.

The problem lies with "Christians." Priorities and desires are changed. Their preferences are not the things of God, but instead they lean more to the things of the world. There is so much to tempt them. We no longer live in a simple world. One cannot keep up with the advances in electronics and other areas, all designed to bring worldly happiness.

Christians don't try to find happiness in God's Word. They turn instead to every attraction the world offers, such as entertainment, hobbies, work, and instant communication with the world through electronic advances.

There's something wrong when we turn to worldly advances and interests, instead of God's Word. Reading about what Christ has done for us should comfort us. It should give us contentment, peace, and that necessary joy. The Word revives us, entertains us, comforts us, heals us, and makes our joy complete.

Our verse in *Ephesians 6:15* speaks of having our feet shod with the preparation of the Gospel of peace. True peace always starts with reconciliation with Christ, brought about by the Gospel message.

We can appreciate that peace more if we sometimes look back to what we were without Christ. *Titus 3:3* gives us a perfect example.

Titus 3:3 For we ourselves also were sometimes foolish, disobedient, deceived, serving divers lusts and pleasures, living in malice and envy, hateful, and hating one another.

This is a perfect example of the world and its enticements. Only Christ can give that deep-settled peace in our hearts that can overcome the world's mindset. The peace of Christ is priceless. It fills us with true joy.

The preparation of the Gospel of peace is designed for the foot, which is the only part of the body to wear a shoe. It's a necessary part of the defensive armor. A long march over sharp stones, mud, wetness, or snow without the proper footwear could cause wounds or pain. Good footwear will enable a soldier to be surefooted and quick to do his duty.

Those that are unprepared or barefoot will probably not complete their mission to bring the Gospel message to others.

The Boots

"Time to go," Glen called. "You got your boots on, Chris?"

The boots were just a bit of a sore point. Chris kept lacing and called out. "I'll be there in a minute." She wondered again why he insisted she have boots instead of her comfortable walking shoes. They didn't even have woman's boots in this heavy brogan lace-up style, but they finally found her a pair in the boy's sizes. Since they came almost to her knees, it took a while to get them on.

It was 4:00 am, and Glen wanted to be in the woods by daybreak, so they drove to his special place to park the truck and set out through the woods to the area he wanted to go. After finding a place for Chris to hunt, Glen continued on alone to his spot.

Chris thought about why she was there, anyway. After Glen's almost fatal-heart attack, he hadn't wanted to give up one of his favorite sports, hunting. Chris just didn't want him out in the woods alone, and most of his hunting buddies were still working, and not available during the week.

Chris knew Glen would be happier if he could continue with some of his favorite things, like hunting, so she said she would just go with him. He gave her a gun and many hours were spent learning about that gun and target practicing. Then she learned about the proper way to hunt. After that came the outfitting with gear and, of course … the boots.

She didn't really want to shoot anything, so she spent the time mostly praying and thinking.

After several hours of peaceful quiet, she saw Glen coming towards her. It had been an unfruitful day for hunting, but it was still beautiful to be out in the woods God had created.

Glen led the way back to the truck. In the daylight, Chris could see just how overgrown and marshy the tiny path was. As she was gazing around the trees, she moved off the path a bit and suddenly sensed something near her foot and looked down.

Horrified, she saw the snake strike her heavy boots halfway between her ankle and her knee. Chris let out a loud squeal, and Glen hurried back. He immediately took aim and fired, shooting the moccasin in the head and killing it.

"You Okay, Honey?"

"Yes," she answered shakily, "You were so right about the boots. That is a pretty big snake. I would have been in bad trouble if I hadn't had these boots on. I also think I'll watch where I'm going next time."

Proverbs 24:27 Prepare thy work without, and make it fit for thyself in the field;...

~~~

Proverbs cautions us to be prepared in what we do. Proverbs is a book of wisdom, and should be used often in our lives.

This little story tells of the importance of wearing the proper footwear for the situation. We can all learn from this, and make sure our Christian lives are properly shod, as well.

That gospel of peace must permeate our very beings to serve as our protection.

A Shattered Life

"I don't know what to do, Mom. Now I've been kicked out of college. I knew better than to take part in those wild sorority initiations, but no one really got hurt. If I could just stop drinking, maybe my head wouldn't be so fuzzy, and I could make better decisions. I can't seem to leave the drinking alone, and it never really helps. My life is a mess, and I'm so unhappy." Vickie sobbed on her mother's shoulder.

"Vickie, you know what I'm going to say, but maybe that's why you came to me, and you just need to hear it again. The first step to complete joy and happiness is to repent and believe the Gospel message. When Jesus forgives you of all your sins, the contentment and peace you will feel will be beyond measure.

"You have to remember, Vickie, the same Gospel which brings peace and joy now will be a torment to you if you don't accept it. On the Day of Judgment, it will be repeated as the heaviest message of condemnation you've ever heard." Mom spoke sternly, trying to make Vickie understand.

"Mom, is it really true? Could there be peace in my heart despite the awful mess I've made of my life?"

"Yes, Honey, remember what Isaiah said in *Isaiah 61:10?*"

Isaiah 61:10 I will greatly rejoice in the LORD, my soul shall be joyful in my God; for he hath clothed me with the garments of salvation,......

"But Mom, I don't want to be miserable and unhappy. What about those who are supposed to be saved, but they are always so grouchy and stern? Why do they always seem so unhappy? You know the ones I mean."

"Yes, Honey, I do. It's very sad that they give the impression to the world that Christians are deprived, straight-laced, and have no joy at all. I often wonder about them because they don't seem to have the joy of the Lord at all.

"Being a Christian is a joyful life, having the peace of God and knowing Heaven will be our eternal home. Peter said it is *'joy unspeakable and full of glory...' 1 Peter 1:8.*

That scripture pretty much says it all. As for other people, Vickie, they will have to answer to God at the Judgment Seat as to the impression they gave others."

Vickie and her mom knelt by the sofa and began to pray.

~~~

How can Christians witness to others when it seems that the love of Christ does not satisfy them? Jesus promises peace and joy to all who come to Him. A Christian's life is a practical testimony to others, without a single word spoken. It has great authority over whether others are saved or not.

They should show others by their actions how wonderful it is to live the Christian life. Is the Christian life abundant life or not? That joy must shine through to others.

Locked Out

It was too early for room service, but they had missed lunch and were all hungry. Janet and Tessa didn't feel like going back out in that heat after finally getting checked in and settled in their rooms.

"Why don't you and Jake go and pick up some food. I know Janet has to rest before going to the first meeting of the conference tonight. We'll just stay here in our room and maybe take a little nap while we wait for you." Tessa used sign language to communicate with them. They all knew someone needed to stay with Janet.

Both Tessa and Janet were deaf, and married to non-hearing impaired husbands. They were all good friends, and in town for a church conference. Janet had suffered a series of strokes and had some mental and physical limitations, but she seemed to enjoy going and being with the others on their travels. None of the others were ready to give up the travel and interests that they now had time for, since they were all retired.

They all agreed about the food, and Jake and Cooper headed out after Jake made sure he had the room key. After they found a place still serving a late lunch, they picked up meals for all of them.

"Cooper, I really appreciate you and Tessa, without your friendship and help with Janet, we wouldn't be able to travel at all. She has such a difficult time." Jake told his friend.

"You know, Jake, you would do the same for us, and we've been friends for a long time." Cooper answered. "I hope the girls are hungry, this lasagna smells great."

"I wonder what's wrong with this key," Jake mused, after trying the lock for the fifth or sixth time. "See if the maid can use her key to let us in."

The maid gladly tried her key, but it wouldn't work, either. "Someone locked the door from the inside! Just knock on the door and they'll open it." She advised.

Jake and Cooper just looked at each other, knowing that because their wives were deaf, they could never hear anyone knock at the door. "You call the front desk, and I'll see if I can find the maintenance man to let us in," said Jake as he walked back down the hall.

After an hour of waiting, they realized the hotel didn't want to get into what they thought was a domestic dispute, where someone locks someone else out of the room. The desk clerks just looked at them, unbelieving, when told that their wives were deaf.

Jake and Cooper calmly sat down on the floor outside of the door and proceeded to eat their cold lunch. They enjoyed a good visit despite the strange looks from the other guests as they passed by.

"It's good we know that God has everything under control, and that He has a reason for everything that happens to us," remarked Jake. "The girls must be taking a good nap and don't even realize how long we've been gone."

Finally they heard someone moving near the door inside the room. Cooper grabbed the food receipt and scrawled quickly. LET US IN! He then slid it under the door to the room. Very quickly the door was opened by a startled Tessa.

"Oh, no," Tessa exclaimed in sign language. "I knew she went to the door, but I didn't know she turned the lock." she signed to them. After they explained, Janet still didn't realize just what she had done.

The desk clerks felt bad when they met the wives, who really were deaf, but they had no way of knowing it was true earlier. Later, by themselves, the clerks discussed how well the guys handled the situation because they were Christians. "Most people would have yelled and threatened to sue us, then would have moved out of the hotel," one remarked.

It was quite funny, looking back on the incident, but it really wasn't very funny at the time to the guys stranded in the hallway.

~~~

Knowing that God is always in the command position, and we are just soldiers trying to follow orders, is sometimes hard to remember, when we go through trying times. Cooper and Jake could have yelled and been very mean to the clerks and the hotel staff. Instead they just made the best of it and showed a calm, gentle spirit to all that were around. It was just an inconvenience. The wives were not in trouble; they were just napping.

Being prepared for whatever life throws at us is the key. A good soldier will always have his boots laced up in preparation for the battle or conflict ahead.

Proverbs 16:1 The preparations of the heart in man, and the answer of the tongue, is from the LORD.

The Irritation

Alan dejectedly looked at his friend. "I think one of the hardest things about getting older is putting up with your children. Why do they think we no longer have any brains and begin to treat us like were two years old? The nagging over and over about a subject that I've already decided upon can be so irritating."

"Well, Joe, perhaps the key is to remember we are still soldiers in this world, and some of the worst things we face are the small irritations that constantly come against us. We have to be prepared to deal with those things, just as much as the big battles.

If we deal with the small irritations improperly, they will turn into huge, gaping wounds in the battle. Preparation is the answer, like lacing those battlefield boots tightly. The small irritations can actually be turned into something of great value when you're prepared to deal with them."

Alan went on, "Remember the only gemstone that starts from a small irritation is a pearl. Some disagree whether the oyster feels pain at the tiny grain of sand that irritates, but most feel that because it is a living creature, it does feel the pain and tries to deal with it by covering it, layer by layer, until it is something beautiful, and no longer painful.

Irritations are what we deal with constantly until we reach Heaven. We must be prepared to deal with them like good soldiers. It's what we go through to reach Heaven. Remember every gate of Heaven is made of…… **'pearl'**. Not diamonds, but pearls guard the entrance way. If we can't deal with the small irritants, how will we ever make it into those magnificent gates that got started by suffering and pain?"

Alan looked at his friend with amazement. "You are so right. I never looked at it that way. These irritations are just another thing we must be constantly prepared for, and know how to deal with each one. Being prepared always comes back to knowing and living what the Word of God instructs us to do."

Revelation 21:21 And the twelve gates were twelve pearls; every several gate was of one pearl:

Change of Plans

Jimmy looked at the cast that was covering his entire leg. He was so upset he didn't even notice the pain from the newly-broken leg. 'How could this have happened now, with the scouts coming Friday night? It completely ends any chance of a college football scholarship. It's the end of my career in football. Why did God let this happen to me?'

The surgeon had said it was such a bad break; it would knock him out of sports for months and months.

"Hi, Jimmy, your mom said to come on in," said Coach Brown as he entered the room. "Well, that's quite a cast. I'm sorry, Jimmy, I know you had lots of hope for a scholarship, and then possibly a career in professional football."

"Sorry, Coach, I probably won't be very good company." Jimmy answered.

"You know, Jimmy, there are other career fields, and you're a good student. I'd like to pray for you and ask God to open another door. I know you used to be a very strong Christian."

"Well, I've been so busy practicing and working to be a good quarterback, I've kind of gotten away from church. Now, I don't know if I even want to go back. Why would God let something like this happen to me? I had my whole life lined up." Jimmy answered with bitter anger in his voice.

"I noticed you haven't been at church much at all," Coach said gently, "I've also noticed you out at the field, putting in hours and hours of extra practice. Sometimes we all get sidetracked from the things that are really important.

"Jimmy, weren't you called into the mission field about three years ago?"

"Yes, but I got into football and just really love that," Jimmy answered.

"There's always room in our lives for sports and other things, but in light of the end time so quickly approaching, perhaps God needs workers in the field a lot worse than He needs football players," Coach gently admonished. "God sometimes allows things to happen to get our attention and get us back on track."

Hebrews 12:5-7 And ye have forgotten the exhortation which speaketh unto you as unto children, My son, despise not thou the chastening of the Lord, nor faint when thou art rebuked of him:
For whom the Lord loveth he chasteneth, and scourgeth every son whom he receiveth. If ye endure chastening, God dealeth with you as with sons; for what son is he whom the father chasteneth not?

Jimmy stared at the coach. "I think I'm going to have to spend some time in prayer, Coach. I didn't realize how far away I am from where I need to be."

Several days later, Jimmy's dad wheeled him into the church in his wheelchair. Coach Brown came up to him. "You're looking good, Jimmy. How are you really doing?"

"I am doing well, Coach, the leg is beginning to mend. Most important of all, spiritually I seem to be getting back on the right track. I want you to know how much I appreciate your coaching me, not just football, but getting my focus back on the important things.

"Remember the Christian college I used to want to go to? I'm applying for a scholastic scholarship there, and it sounds like I have a pretty good chance of getting it."

Chapter Seven

Shield of Faith

Ephesians 6:16 Above all, taking the shield of faith, wherewith ye shall be able to quench all the fiery darts of the wicked

    The shield refers to the large piece of armor the soldier held in front of him to fend off weapons of every kind. It could have been rectangular or oval, and usually it was large enough to reach from his chin down to his knees. He could kneel behind it and deflect arrows, or stand shield-to-shield with other soldiers, making a solid wall of protection for safety.

    The shield would be made of two layers of wood adhered together, covered with linen and leather and then bound with iron. It would easily extinguish and deflect all the fiery darts that were shot at him.

    Satan uses a different kind of dart and arrow, the fiery darts of the tongues of men to torment the mind and cause doubts, hurt, and disappointment. He hopes to destroy us using methods such as these.

    The shield is held over the center of the body. The heart is also in the center of our body. It is vital to our life as a Christian. We cannot live without our heart beating inside of us, and we cannot exist as Christians without the shield of faith to protect us.

    The Christian faith forms this shield of protection for us. This easily counteracts any darts thrown by the enemy, putting out the flames to keep them from spreading. Faith is required in our Christian lives. We cannot please God without it. ***Hebrews 11:6.*** It protects and keeps us from being overwhelmed by the adversity that surrounds us.

When we look closely at the patriarchs of faith mentioned in **Hebrews 11**, we realize it's not who they were, but it's what they did! All were just average people with tremendous God-given abilities because of the way they obeyed God and lived their lives by faith. They had faults, they were human, but faith controlled their lives.

Faith is a process, just as the Christian life is a process. We cannot live on our past history. It's not what I have done, but what I am doing. It doesn't matter if we had faith at a certain time in the past. That doesn't affect whether we have faith today. Faith is ongoing and continuous.

The shield is to defend every part of the body, not just one part. The helmet covers the head, the breastplate the heart and vital organs, but the shield was large, and if not large enough to cover the entire body, the soldier could move it to deflect the arrows or darts, wherever they were aimed, just as faith can defend attacks directed towards any part of us. Faith protects all of the Christian.

You could say the shield is outer armor. The body is already protected. The head is covered by the helmet, and the chest with the breastplate, the girdle for the loins; the shield would protect the attack from ever getting close to the inner armor. The shield not only protects the entire body, but it protects the other pieces of armor. Perhaps this is why it is '*above all*'.

The Christian must have true faith, and not a shoddy counterfeit. Some think they can accept Christ and have faith in a simple speaking of words, and just having head knowledge instead of heart knowledge. If one has not been humbled and crushed by their personal sin, completely convicted that Jesus is the only solution, and therefore repent from the depth of their heart, they will wind up with just head knowledge, but will not have heart knowledge, and the strength of the shield of faith will not be available to them.

Their faith will be flimsy, easy to crush, and so very weak that it will fail at the first test. True, heartfelt repentance and forgiveness from Christ must be the prerequisite for a strong faith that will stand. There is no way to accept Christ fully except by faith. Faith and Salvation are bonded together.

Contentment and Faith

Faith must be strong and be kept strong. A Christian who is calm and content, and not drastically affected by problems, hardships or whatever, will have a stronger faith than the weaker Christian who waivers when the storms come. Paul said he had learned to be content in whatever state he was in. *Philippians 4:11*. We must also be content.

Do you notice that a strong person is not as affected by the changes in the weather, whether cold or hot or stormy? Yet, one that is not healthy is very much affected by their surrounding conditions.

Keeping oneself strong in Christ takes a determined effort of prayer, reading the Word, and being obedient to all that is required of one who follows Him. Strength will surround you in all circumstances you find yourself in if you have committed yourself to follow Him closely.

Contentment means a willingness to wait on answers from Christ. Weak faith wants instant answers or the person thinks God didn't hear, or God doesn't love them. A contented Christian knows God is working, even when they cannot see it. They know God sometimes says "Not now, wait!" They also know God sometimes says, "No!!" Since He knows the end from the beginning, He always knows what is best for us. Trust is part of contentment.

Temptations, Trials and Faith

All Christians are tempted. All Christians are tried. How we respond to those temptations and trials depends on how strong our faith is.

How hard is it for you to break from temptations, to ride out the trials? In a net, a little fish will be held securely, while a large fish can often break through to freedom. Are you a small fish in faith, or a strong one that can break through?

Peter speaks of the trial of manifold temptations. *I Peter 1:6-9*. How precious it is to the Lord when our faith is stronger than any temptation, and our faith is purified by withstanding, even though it was tried with fire. Remaining faithful to Him in the trial will result in praise, glory, and honor to Christ and ourselves.

Our scripture in *Ephesians 6:16* tells us about quenching the fiery darts of the wicked. It doesn't say maybe you will be able to withstand and stop some of the enemy's darts, but it says:

'Ye shall be able to quench all the fiery darts of the wicked'.

There is no question about it. If you take the shield of faith properly, you will resist, repel, and stop everything Satan can throw at you. Not just ordinary trials and temptations, but **all** that comes against you.

It would be well to note that the scripture calls him wicked. Remember he is totally evil, the opposite of all that is holy and true. We must completely hate him. If you indulge in sin or sinful things, you look just like him! He is evil, black and dark; the complete opposite of all that describes Christ.

In the heart of each and every person there is a tendency to sin. It is Satan who does the tempting, but James said it is our own lust that draws us into sin.

James 1:14. But every man is tempted, when he is drawn away of his own lust, and enticed.

This human inclination can be denied and fought with our spiritual weapons, and it can be overcome.

The desire to fight or to succumb is our choice. We might be successful at avoiding a temptation and keeping our distance from it. Avoiding the battle is probably only temporary. Satan knows our weaknesses, and until we learn to stand and fight and overcome the enemy, the same temptation will return. Once we have the victory over a situation, it will be easier to win the next battle.

Carelessness cannot be tolerated when temptation is concerned. A small child can burn down an entire house by playing with matches. Never dabble in the things that can cause you to fall. Avoid them entirely, and keep your weapons ready for the fight.

Remember the shield of faith is able to cover your entire body, and even cover the other pieces of the armor. Is your shield the shield of faith or one of paper? The shield that is able to protect and keep you comes from God above, the very maker of faith. Keep this shield close to you and ready to use.

Faith and Fear

If Satan finds he cannot capture a Christian by temptation, he will often attack him with fear. We sometimes call this anxiety and worry. Faith alone can quench the fiery dart of fear, even when it comes by worry or anxiety. There always seems to be something that causes nail-biting in our world.

Faith helps us to remember what God has done in the past, and all His promises to help in any situation. We can always count on Him.

Only Believe

Johnny shook his head, "You're just wasting your time, Chaplin. There is no hope for me. I killed two men, remember? When they strap me in that chair next week and pull the switch, it's all over. If there is a Hell, that's where I'll be. There's no way God would ever forgive me for what I've done."

"Johnny," Chaplain Carson implored, "Do you believe that the Bible is true, that it's the Word of God?"

Johnny wearily replied, "Yeah, but it's just too late for me. Why can't you understand? I was raised right, but I turned my back on God and all He stands for when I went on that drunken rampage. I actually turned my back on Him years before that even happened. God wouldn't come into this sinful place. He wouldn't have anything to do with me."

"Johnny, you are wrong! It is never too late for anyone to ask God to save them. That's why He came into this world, remember? He came to save that which was lost! He didn't come just to answer the prayers of good people. We all have sinned and come short of the glory of God! There are no big sins that He cannot forgive. That's why He died on the Cross. For me **and** for you! Please let me share a few scriptures with you."

At Johnny's nod, the chaplain opened his Bible and shared the plan of salvation. He ended with the following verses.

Hebrews 7:25 Wherefore he is able also to save them to the uttermost that come unto God by him, seeing he ever liveth to make intercession for them.

Jeremiah 31:34b ………….. Know the LORD: for they shall all know me, from the least of them unto the greatest

of them, saith the LORD: for I will forgive their iniquity, and I will remember their sin no more.

"Are you sure, Chaplain? Are you really sure He could forgive me, even as mean as I am?"

Chaplain Carson said, "I'm positive, Johnny. There is nothing He won't forgive if you really mean it from the heart. You'll still have to pay the penalty to society for what you have done, but Jesus will be waiting with open arms to welcome you to that heavenly home."

Johnny bowed down on his knees, and with tears streaming down his face, he asked God for forgiveness for what he had done. He then asked the chaplain to call his parents and tell them that he had been forgiven. Peace and joy entered his heart like he had never known, and he knew he could face the next few days, because he was no longer alone.

Communication Broken

Brad and Anita felt very weary after the wind finally let up and the rain slowed to a steady drizzle. The twins cried for attention and breakfast. Anita went to see what she could do. She had powdered formula, jars of fruit, and a fairly good supply of diapers. They also had plenty of emergency jugs of water. Their important needs would be met for a while.

Brad went outside to check how bad the damage was and see if he could get a signal of any kind on his cell phone. Several trees were down, and one window was smashed, and lots of shingles were missing from the roof.

They had no neighbors close by, so he wasn't sure about the damage to others in the area. He could see that the only road out was underwater. The river banks just couldn't absorb the torrential rains of the past two days. All of the surrounding low areas would be flooded until the water went down.

There was no signal at all on the cell phone, and with the power out, Brad and Anita felt very isolated. Storms and relentless, flooding rain had cut off all communication. Brad had a wind-up emergency radio, but most of the stations within the area were off the air.

That afternoon Brad and Anita thanked God for His protection of their family and their home. They would find out soon that hundreds were without homes, and there were many lives lost as the storms moved through the area. They didn't have any current communications, but they knew it would be restored as soon as possible.

Faith in God causes us to walk in perfect peace, no matter what comes against us. He is more than able to handle any situation, even those that are far beyond our capabilities to handle. God's mercy reigns in any situation. Faith helps us to see and comprehend that mercy.

How completely we depend on phones, TVs, radios, and other gadgets that constantly keep us in touch with each other and the world around us.

In disasters, man-made electronics can stop working and be out of commission. We can adapt and survive loss of electrical power, but what would we do without communication with God?

If somehow the resource of prayer and God's Word were to be removed from our lives, how empty would life be! Without a church to help us mature and grow, without a pastor to bring anointed messages, how devastated and helpless we could become.

In many countries, Bibles are not allowed. There are no Christian churches, and meeting together with believers could be punished by death, or years in a dark prison cell. But in that darkest, most remote dungeon, Jesus lives in the hearts of the believers.

Talking to God in prayer cannot be taken away from the Christian. The Bibles might be destroyed, but if you have buried the Word in your heart, the Word will return to your memory as it is needed. It can never be lost, and therefore you can never lose your contact and communication with the one who really is in control, our heavenly Father.

2 Corinthians 4:7-10   But we have this treasure in earthen vessels, that the excellency of the power may be of God, and not of us.
We are troubled on every side, yet not distressed; we are perplexed, but not in despair;
Persecuted, but not forsaken; cast down, but not destroyed; Always bearing about in the body the dying of the Lord Jesus, that the life also of Jesus might be made manifest in our body.

In the Midst of It All

Jan clutched the lab request, the prescription, and other papers in her hand as she left the doctor's office in the August heat. As she got into her car, she thought to herself, "I still think it's an inner ear infection. Why on earth didn't they just give me a shot of medicine? That cleared one up years ago."

All these tests will probably be thousands of dollars' worth. Now I'll have to wait and fight the dizziness another two weeks to get all these medical tests done and get the results back to the doctor.'

"Lord, I promised to trust you, and I do! But I know you understand this struggle, I need to work to pay the bills, but it's so difficult when I stay dizzy and sick all the time. You know it's not even safe to drive, but it's so hard to find someone that is free to take me. Sometimes it seems like I'm just in a dark tunnel, and I can't see the way out."

The frustration increased the next day as Jan realized she couldn't take the prescribed medication. It knocked her out completely for hours, and then made it impossible to function with a heavy, drugged feeling when she did wake up.

Several days later, she entered her small home office and attempted to catch up on some of the things she was behind on. As usual, it was very difficult to focus on the computer screen, and the numerous dizzy spells continued to plague her.

Because she had to have fasting blood work done that morning, she realized she entirely missed her regular devotional time.

Knowing she needed to talk to the Father more than anything, Jan went to her prayer corner and sank down on her knees. Arising after a while, she opened her Bible and found several scriptures.

1 Peter 4:12, 13 Beloved, think it not strange concerning the fiery trial which is to try you, as though some strange thing happened unto you:
But rejoice, inasmuch as ye are partakers of Christ's sufferings; that, when his glory shall be revealed, ye may be glad also with exceeding joy.

Jan then turned to *John 1*.

John 1:4,5 In him was life; and the life was the light of men.
And the light shineth in darkness; and the darkness comprehended it not.

With praise in her heart, Jan returned to her work. She had a renewed confidence that God was in complete control, and all she had to do was believe Him. She also knew she could trust Him completely, no matter what the outcome might be.

Weeks later, Jan gave up on having more tests. She had learned to cope with the problems, and jokingly called it her 'new normal'. Although the doctor still had a laundry list of other tests for her to have done, she told him she simply couldn't afford it, and had decided to completely trust God to heal whatever it was.

The 'dizzy spells' still happened occasionally, but not often. The nausea disappeared with the dizzy spells. She was using the computer with only minor focusing problems. Most of all, she knew God had given her the peace that He would take care of her.

Lies

"It's all a lie, Carl! Mona just made that up because she was angry with me. You know I had to fire her as my secretary several months ago. She really didn't do a good job, and couldn't keep up with everything in the office. But I didn't kill that girl. I didn't even leave the bar with her. I just walked her to her car.

Mona made it all up about seeing us drive off together." Alex implored Carl to believe him.

"Alex, they found your fingerprints on that drink napkin in the floorboard, also on the dash and seats," countered Carl. "If you want me to defend you, I've got to know the absolute truth, so there won't be surprises at the trial."

"I did get in the car, but I just sat there five or ten minutes before I got out and drove home in my car. She drove off immediately and I went home. I have no witnesses because I live alone, and the neighbors were too far away to even see me. I didn't kill her, Carl. You know me, and you know I wouldn't do that."

Carl pondered a minute and said, "Let's talk a minute about that, Alex. I used to know you quite well. We belong to the same church; we graduated from law school together. I haven't seen you in church in months. You decline all our invitations to get together. What happened, Alex?"

"I'm not real sure, Carl. Last year, my client in the Parker trial gave me a bottle of wine when we won his case. I started to refuse it, but didn't. It all started with just a little glass of wine at night, just to relax, then I began drinking more and more, and it seemed to control my life. Before I knew it, I couldn't quit. I'm probably an alcoholic, but I'm not a killer.

"I usually was ashamed and would only drink at home, but for some reason I went by the bar that night, and Mona was there with Tina. Tina got to talking to me about her problems. That's all that happened. I didn't kill her, Carl. Mona is just trying to get revenge.

"I've had too much guilt about the drinking to go to church. The truth is, I didn't want to give it up. Now I know I'll never touch another drop, and I've prayed for God to forgive me, deliver me from the bondage, and help me once again."

"I believe you, Alex. So far, there has been no weapon found, and the evidence is just circumstantial, but that lie could really be convincing to a jury.

"You can't leave your apartment now to go to church, but I'd like to give you some scriptures to study, and ask the pastor to come by and see you. Is that okay?"

"Yes, absolutely, I picked up my Bible, but I just couldn't even remember where to begin," Alex answered gratefully.

"These scriptures all refer to Christ being our shield. Study these. and then I'm sure they will lead you to others that you need."

Psalms 3:3 But thou, O LORD, art a shield for me; my glory, and the lifter up of mine head.
Psalms 33:20 Our soul waiteth for the LORD: he is our help and our shield.
Deuteronomy 33:29 Happy art thou, O Israel: who is like unto thee, O people saved by the LORD, the shield of thy help, and who is the sword of thy excellency! and thine enemies shall be found liars unto thee; and thou shalt tread upon their high places.

Several weeks later, Carl called Alex. "Alex, I have great news! Tina had an unhappy ex-boyfriend. The weapon was found in his garage. The DNA evidence will be further proof, but most important is the fact that he has confessed. It proves your story, and you are now completely absolved of any guilt in the case."

"Oh, Carl, that is great news. I'll look forward to getting back to work and, most important, getting back to church. God has already given me complete peace that it all is in His hands, but it's good to hear that it will all be resolved publicly.

"I've found the key to fighting the battles and the temptations like alcohol. It's just simply staying very close to God by prayer, reading the Word, and having the support of other believers. Thank you, Carl, for helping me and believing in me."

Chapter Eight

Helmet of Salvation

Ephesians 6:17a And take the helmet of salvation,...

To 'take' means to receive or accept; just as we would receive our salvation from Jesus. Other parts of the soldier's armor would have been laid out for him, but the helmet would have been handed to him by his armor bearer.

It would have been made of bronze, possibly with leather attachments.

The helmet is another vital piece of defensive armor. It helps to defend us, but it doesn't protect us from suffering.

How very vital and important it is to protect the head. Workers wear hard hats; even children wear helmets for protection on their bicycles. Brain injuries have become a specialized field of medicine. We know how devastating injuries to the head can be.

Satan loves to aim for the mind, and control Christians by their thoughts. Probably our minds are more exposed to his attacks than any other part of us.

As the helmet protects the head, salvation protects the soul of man and gives him everlasting life, instead of everlasting torment.

The helmet of salvation is a gift from God, provided by Him like the rest of our armor. God provided this helmet to protect the intricate mind of man, which He created. Salvation is God's gift to protect against the power of sin.

....and for an helmet, the hope of salvation 1 Thess. 5:8b.

Salvation also is our hope of final deliverance from sin when we make Heaven our home. It is the promise of the things we have not yet fully received. Our salvation fortifies us and diminishes the bondage of the past.

Salvation is available to everyone. All anyone needs to do is call out to Him. The invitation is to everyone on the earth. The greatest desire the Lord has is that all would be saved.

Isaiah 45:22 Look unto me, and be ye saved, all the ends of the earth: for I am God, and there is none else.

2 Peter 3:9 The Lord is not slack concerning his promise, as some men count slackness; but is longsuffering to us-ward, not willing that any should perish, but that all should come to repentance.

Salvation is based upon faith and believing. God never forces Himself on anyone.

Acts 16:30, 31 And brought them out, and said, Sirs, what must I do to be saved?
And they said, Believe on the Lord Jesus Christ, and thou shalt be saved, and thy house.

Once a person is saved, it is necessary to continue to stay close to Christ, continue to believe on Him, and continue to live their lives according to God's Word.

Ezekiel 18:24 But when the righteous turneth away from his righteousness, and committeth iniquity, and doeth according to all the abominations that the wicked man doeth, shall he live? All his righteousness that he hath done shall not be mentioned: in his trespass that he hath trespassed, and in his sin that he hath sinned, in them shall he die.

There Must Be an Order

"But Ben, I don't understand why. You get to lead the opening prayer and lead the singing, and most of the other guys are asked to help, also. Brother Sims has never asked me to do anything, not even take up the offering.

I've been coming to the church and the youth meetings for almost a year now and I'd like to participate like the others do."

"Caleb," Ben slowly and prayerfully answered, "God has an order, a perfect order in the way things are done for Him. Have you noticed any main differences in yourself and most of the rest of us?"

"Well, you all do seem to enjoy the services more, and you go to the altar a lot, and things like that," Caleb answered.

"Do you remember all the messages we've had about surrendering everything to God and getting saved?" Ben asked carefully.

"Oh, that. Well, I'm just a real good person and I never felt like any of that applied to me. I mean really, do you honestly think God would send anyone to hell?

"My folks say there really isn't a hell, anyway. It's just kind of scare tactics by the church to keep control over everyone." Caleb shook his head as he answered.

Ben gently answered. "Caleb, everything in the Bible tells how man originated in sin and remained in sin until they turned to God."

Romans 3:23 For all have sinned, and come short of the glory of God;

"How many times have we been taught, or listened to messages that told how Jesus, God's very Son, who was born without sin, loved us sinners so much that He gave his own life to die on the Cross that we might believe upon Him and be saved from our sin. I know you've heard that."

John 3:16,17 For God so loved the world, that he gave his only begotten Son, that whosoever believeth in him should not perish, but have everlasting life.
For God sent not his Son into the world to condemn the world; but that the world through him might be saved

"Remember I said God has an order, and we have to stay with the order of God? Brother Sims cannot use you until a few things have happened.

"First, you must know that God does not dwell in an unclean temple, one that hasn't been cleansed from sin.

"You can't be used of God until He comes to dwell in your heart. It is necessary to first acknowledge sin and admit that you are a sinner.

"Then you need to confess your sin to Him and repent of that sin, and ask Him to come into your heart. Caleb, God will gladly come into your life and change you from a sinner into a child of God.

"Once this has been done, Brother Sims will see the change in you, and will gladly use you to help in the services. Of course, you have to do what is necessary to remain a Christian, like reading the Word, praying and attending church services faithfully. It's necessary to resist temptation to blend right back into the world.

"Christians are different! The Bible says we are a peculiar people. We try to not look and act like the world, because that is Satan's territory."

"You're right, Ben, I just never thought of it that way before. I'm going to the altar tonight and surrender all that I am to God. I really do believe in Heaven and I want to be saved."

Beauty in the Midst

He walked on in the early morning, the brown, crunchy grass under his feet. Once again it was cold, with an icy wind whistling against his face. The bare trees, like gray sentinels standing in the gray dawn, made the path slightly formidable and unpredictable.

He lived so far south, snow was rarely seen. He often thought it would have been a welcome change from the dreary cold grays and browns of the winter. But he knew even the pretty, white snow that fell further north would soon turn dingy yellow and brown as it melted and settled with the contaminants in the air.

Somehow this morning the cold grayness didn't seem so chilling after the total recommitment to Christ last night. He remembered the subject of pastor's message, "Battlefields", and how we are all living in enemy-occupied territory.

Listening to that message, he knew immediately that he had given up after the death of his wife. He quit praying, quit reading the Word, and gave in to the dreariness, day after day, of just staring at the television. Nothing was the same without her.

He knew only darkness of the mind. He no longer looked for joy or happiness, and it stayed far from him. Church became optional; he only went if he really felt like it. He had given Satan a wide open door to come into his depressed mind.

He had felt such an urgency to go to the church last night, and now he knew why. Jesus was fighting for his very soul, even when he had given up fighting for himself. Somehow in that depressed state, he didn't even realize he had given place to the devil and quit fighting to stay alive spiritually.

As the sun arose, he felt his spirit also lift as he prayed for family and friends and strength to continue the fight. The sun revealed now and then an evergreen in the forest of gray, skeletal trees.

The winter birds called and began their day. Squirrels scurried from limb to limb and ran through the dead leaves to dig up acorns buried weeks earlier. The sun warmed the dreary landscape, and he raised his hands in praise as contentment and peace once again flooded his soul.

Isaiah 61:3 To appoint unto them that mourn in Zion, to give unto them beauty for ashes, the oil of joy for mourning, the garment of praise for the spirit of heaviness; that they might be called trees of righteousness, the planting of the LORD, that he might be glorified

~~~

There is a beauty even in the starkness of winter when you choose to live close to the giver of life and have the rivers of living water flowing deep within your soul.

Life can be difficult. At those times, draw closer to the Lord, not further away. He has the balm of Gilead to soothe your troubled soul.

Psalms 24:1 The earth is the LORD'S, and the fulness thereof; the world, and they that dwell therein.

He Must Increase

"Your mail, General Parker," announced his aide as he placed the pack of correspondence on the general's desk.

"Thank you, Private Curran, would you bring me some coffee in fifteen minutes?"

"Yes, sir," answered the private as he exited the room.

The general picked up his wife's letter. It really seemed strange to receive a written letter, as they usually talked by the telephone or the internet. He felt a twinge of apprehension as he opened the envelope.

"Gerald, I'm so sorry to tell you like this," she began. "I just couldn't tell you on the phone, and email wouldn't do, either. This won't be good news, but it has to be told. I really hate to hit you with everything at once, but it's just the way it happened.

First of all, the children: Heidi had a wreck and totaled her car. She wasn't hurt and only a tree was involved, but her blood-alcohol level was far too high, and she has lost her license, as well as needing to do thirty hours of community service.

Joseph will have to return to the rehab or go to jail, since he was caught purchasing more drugs. He leaves in the morning.

That leaves me. I wanted to wait until your tour was over and tell you in person, but since you've extended for another six months, I'll have to tell you like this. I can no longer be the wife you want me to be. The loneliness is more than I can bear.

There have been several affairs over the years, but I got sick of that, too. I want the freedom to find someone who wants to be with me permanently, instead of being married to the military service. You well know we've drifted further and further apart and I don't believe there is anything left of our marriage to salvage. The most hurtful thing to me has been your affair with your career. It has always seemed to exclude us.

We've been terrible parents, you were always gone and I couldn't do it by myself. Perhaps we can handle this quietly so it will not hinder your career. My attorney will be contacting you." The letter was simply signed, "Judy."

In the same packet of mail, Gerald noticed the thick envelope with the name of a prominent attorney in their hometown.

Hot tears formed in Gerald's eyes as he bent his head and cupped his hand over his face. It was all true. He had concentrated so much on qualifying for the next promotion, he had excluded his family from his life.

During the last 15 years, he had volunteered for every position that would advance his career, regardless of where it was or what his family needed. Now he had lost everything. The career did not seem to matter when he faced the loss of his wife and children.

"Your coffee, sir." Gerald hadn't heard the aide return to his office and he stared at him blankly with a tear-stained face.

"Forgive me, sir, you've obviously had a shock of some kind. I'd like to help if I can. Would you allow me to share what helps me through some of the most devastating times in my life?"

"I need help, Private Curran. For perhaps the first time in my life, this situation is beyond any capabilities I have."

Private Curran stepped outside the office and reached for the Bible on his desk. He returned to the general's office and quietly shut the door behind him. He opened the Word to **Psalms 46:1** and began to share.

God is our refuge and strength, a very present help in trouble

God used a private who was low in military rank to share his Word to a general. Our position in this life really has nothing to do with where we are in the body of Christ. In *2 Kings 5* we are told the story of Namaan and how he was healed and came to God. Note in verse two it tells of the captive maid.

2 Kings 5:2,3 And the Syrians had gone out by companies, and had brought away captive out of the land of Israel a little maid; and she waited on Naaman's wife. And she said unto her mistress, Would God my lord were with the prophet that is in Samaria! for he would recover him of his leprosy

She was just a little captive maid, but she was free in Christ and she was a great missionary. Don't ever let your worldly position either puff you up or pull you down. Where you are in Christ is the most important. Can He use you where you are?

Silent Struggle

Laura awoke when her niece patted her shoulder. "Call me when you get sleepy. I'll get Ginger to sit with you."

For days, they had been alternating sitting with Ella. They knew she was dying and they had taken on the sad task to be with her for what they had been told would just be a few hours, but the time stretched into days.

Now they were all exhausted. Ella was in a coma and not communicating. She seemed so peaceful and pain-free, but still she lingered, puzzling the doctor and the hospice nurses. Not sure why she was holding on, the nurse asked each of them if there was anything they needed to tell Ella, or any final promise to make. None of them could think of anything.

Ginger didn't get up to sit with Laura. Instead, she stayed on the cot, sleeping, after her sister called her. They were all so exhausted.

After praying that God would reveal anything she needed to do or say to her sister, Laura opened up her Bible and read by the tiny glow of the small lamp. She turned first to Luke and read the story of Lazarus. It was comforting that God would send the angels to carry one into Heaven.

Luke 16:22 *And it came to pass, that the beggar died, and was carried by the angels into Abraham's bosom*:

The Psalms came to mind and Laura found herself reading in chapter 72.

V. 4 …. he shall save the children of the needy..

The words seemed to burn into her mind. Suddenly, she knew! She knew exactly why her sister was lingering. Ella was a great prayer warrior. She called her children's and grandchildren's names in prayer every day, and often several times a day. Most were still not saved.

Laura knew her sister well, and she also knew there was no one else in her family that would faithfully take on that burden of prayer daily for each and every one.

It was so important to Ella to be together again with her children in Heaven. Even though she didn't speak a word, Laura knew Ella wanted her to tell her family that if they wanted to see her again, they would need to accept Christ and live a Christian life. She also knew Ella was asking her to take on the burden of praying for them to be saved.

Laura grasped her sister's hand and leaned close to her face. "Yes, dear sister, yes! I will tell them; and I will pray for them."

Wiping her tears, Laura felt a complete peace. She knew that was exactly what Ella wanted her to do.

Suddenly, an awesome, glowing presence filled the room, along with a soft, beautiful sound. Laura knew the angels had arrived to carry her sister home.

"Girls," she called, "it's time." They gathered around the bed, murmuring their last goodbyes.

Later, Laura asked them, "Did you see anything?" They all agreed they definitely felt something in the room, but were helpless to explain what. Ginger said when she was called to get up with Laura, she felt like something was holding her to the cot, and she could not rise.

"Yes," Laura confirmed, "I needed to promise her something. I needed to be alone to pray and read."

Laura asked the pastor to share at the funeral service about the family accepting Christ if they wished to be with Ella again.

He in turn asked her to share the happenings of that final hour with the assembled family and friends. It was difficult for her, but she knew God would help her to tell exactly the way it happened. And He did.

Psalms 116:15 Precious in the sight of the LORD is the death of his saints.

Written in the memory of my dear sister, Ina Mae... 8/1/1928 - 9/16/2009 I'm still praying, Sis.

Chapter Nine

Sword of the Spirit

E*phesians 6:17b ...and the sword of the Spirit, which is the word of God:*

All of the defensive weapons that we've spoken of can help you to stand your ground and hold off Satan, but here is an *offensive* weapon that will cause the enemy to leave! That weapon is the Sword of the Spirit, which is the Word of God. It is also used for defense when under attack.

Perhaps the sword is the most necessary piece of the soldiers armor. To be a soldier, he must have a sword. A wise soldier will be careful in the use of his sword.

If not in combat, a sword should remain in its sheath, always ready to be used. When in the midst of the battle, he would use the sword to fight, and the same sword could be used in rescue to cut a fellow soldier loose from his bindings.

Paul wrote of the short, two-edged weapon used in hand-to-hand combat. Spiritually, this refers to the same Word that Jesus used when facing his tempter.

A soldier must have a sword, and he must be skilled in the use of this weapon, in the same way a Christian must know God's Word and know how to apply it.

Matthew 4:4 But he answered and said, It is written, Man shall not live by bread alone, but by every word that proceedeth out of the mouth of God.

The weapons a Christian uses are not the carnal warlike weapons of the world, but they are spiritual, just like the battles we face. Every weapon we are told to use is found in the Word of God. The Word is always the key. Descriptions of each weapon are located there, and the use of each is described. Any weapon that does not point directly to God's Word should be discarded and never used.

As you apply yourself to comprehensive study of the Bible, it will become very clear just how each weapon is used in the different battles we face. God's Word is our legacy, our wealth, and our riches. Hide it in your heart. It is constantly needed. It is stronger than any hindrance or failing the enemy might throw at us. Remember, Satan uses our weaknesses to defeat us. He is no match for the truth of God's Word.

It might be the weakness of pride, greed, deceitfulness, laziness or lust. Whatever your own personal weakness is, use the powerful Word of God to overcome it and become a victorious Christian.

Learn how to use and apply God's Word to any situation. Only by reading, studying, memorizing, and then quoting it out loud do you overcome the wiles of the enemy.

There is no need for any other offensive weapon. Like the sword, the Word must be grasped firmly in the hand of the believer and used with skill.

As long as the Word is buried in a believer's heart, the Holy Spirit will give the Christian the appropriate Word needed for the particular battle he is involved in.

Love the Word, read it, memorize it. It's good to read books about the Bible, but that must never take the place of reading the Bible itself.

Hebrews 4:12 *For the word of God is quick, and powerful, and sharper than any two edged sword, piercing even to the dividing asunder of soul and spirit, and of the joints and marrow, and is a discerner of the thoughts and intents of the heart.*

In our battles, the Word can lay bare any lies, and separate the false from the true. The Word brings judgment. It shows the way to salvation. We know the Lord used the Word in temptations. ***Matthew 4:1-10***. We can use the Word with all assurance and power to defend from the enemy's attacks.

Notice that Paul mentions all the other weapons before he mentions the sword. They are all necessary, and should be in place before the sword is to be used.

If the Word is used before salvation, it is often misquoted, misused, and often used to promote ungodly things. Some put on their own righteousness instead of the righteousness of God. Those without faith often tempt God to prove Himself.

Satan knows God's Word. He will often use portions of a scripture, or add something to it to try to convince someone to do his will. Only through our own knowledge of the Word can we refute his horrible tactics.

In the hands of an assailant, a sword could be deadly to the innocent and unarmed. The Word in the mouth of evil people can only hurt themselves and others that do not know the Word.

Satan is a spirit, and as such we must fight him with spiritual weapons. This is why the sword is likened to the Word, which is the strongest spiritual weapon we have.

2 Corinthians 10:3-5 For though we walk in the flesh, we do not war after the flesh:
(For the weapons of our warfare are not carnal, but mighty through God to the pulling down of strong holds;)
Casting down imaginations, and every high thing that exalteth itself against the knowledge of God, and bringing into captivity every thought to the obedience of Christ;

We live and walk in this world in a body of flesh and blood, but it is through the mind that we know, we understand, we think, and we imagine. Our mind is the battlefield of the enemy! The mind must be guarded by the Holy Spirit of God. We walk in the flesh, but we do not fight in the flesh.

Ephesians 6:12 For we wrestle not against flesh and blood, but against principalities, against powers, against the rulers of the darkness of this world, against spiritual wickedness in high places.

The enemy loves to inject corrupt thoughts into our minds, or place seeds of doubt that can lead to strongholds. He tells lies that affect relationships with others. The Word is the spiritual sword that overcomes the enemy of Christ.

The Word Is Vital

"Hi, Crystal, is it more wedding decisions we need to discuss?"

"Not this time, Paul," Crystal laughed. "I just wondered if you'd like to go to the Bible study this evening. It means a lot to me."

Paul squirmed, searching his mind for an excuse. "Um..., well, no, not tonight, Honey. I better get to work on straightening that back room so the things can be moved."

Paul always went with Crystal to church on Sunday morning, but he had never studied the Bible much, and felt very uncomfortable in a group discussing it. He felt it was enough that he had made his commitment to Christ.

That evening, shortly after 7:00, Paul received a frantic call from Crystal's dad. "We've got to get to the hospital right away, an accident. We'll see you there."

Paul hurriedly drove the ten miles to the ER. When he arrived, he quickly found her family. "What happened? She was just on her way to the church."

Crystal's dad answered, "She swerved suddenly to avoid a boy on a bicycle and rammed into a large cement truck. No one else was hurt, but she's pretty bad, from what the doctor briefly told us. They took her into surgery."

Several hours later, the surgeon came into the waiting room. The room by then was filled with other family members, church friends, and the pastor and his wife.

"She remains in critical condition, and what happens in the next twelve hours will determine if she lives or not. We've done everything we can do. The immediate family can see her very briefly. It will be some time before she wakes up, if all goes well."

When Paul and her parents came out of the room, he slumped over in a corner chair. The pastor came and grasped his hands. "Paul, when we've done all we can do, then we have to stand on God's Word and trust Him to bring it to pass. All of us that are saved are soldiers in this world. *Ephesians 6:10-17.* All soldiers must have a sword, which is the powerful Word of God. It's the strongest spiritual weapon we have, and we must be very knowledgeable of how to use it."

"That's just it, Pastor, I've never read the Bible much at all. I don't know very many scriptures and wouldn't have any idea where to turn to for help."

Pastor opened his Bible and said, "Let me share a couple with you, and I'll write some others down for you to look up."

1 Peter 2:24 Who his own self bare our sins in his own body on the tree, that we, being dead to sins, should live unto righteousness: by whose stripes ye were healed.
James 5:14-16 Is any sick among you? let him call for the elders of the church; and let them pray over him, anointing him with oil in the name of the Lord:
And the prayer of faith shall save the sick, and the Lord shall raise him up; and if he have committed sins, they shall be forgiven him.
Confess your faults one to another, and pray one for another, that ye may be healed. The effectual fervent prayer of a righteous man availeth much.

Most of the friends and family left for the night, but Paul and Crystal's parents remained in the waiting room, praying and reading the Word.

Paul was amazed how the Word seemed to come alive and speak directly to him. He knew he would always love to read and study the Word in the future.

About midmorning, the doctor came out and told them she was improving, and with some recovery time would probably fully recover. The family was elated and so relieved to hear this.

Paul knew he had gained a priceless treasure in those long hours; a treasure that would become a part of who he was and would be forever.

John 1:1 In the beginning was the Word, and the Word was with God, and the Word was God.

Regrets

Patrick remembered that moment just before leaving. He was packing his small carry-on bag and briefcase and picked up his small Bible. The carry-on was really full, and the briefcase was full of notes and the presentation for the meeting.

He put the Bible back on the nightstand, thinking that the hotel would have a Bible, and it wasn't necessary to have it on the plane with him.

Now that scene flashed in his mind. The pilot had announced an emergency, and one engine was out. They were losing altitude. Many of the passengers were beginning to panic. Some tried to pray and asked if others would pray for them. Many asked if anyone had a Bible with them.

Patrick didn't have his Bible. His thoughts searched frantically for scriptures that would help, but none came to mind.

Finally as the plane continued to careen and fly erratically, he remembered his favorites and began to loudly quote from John.

John 3:16,17 For God so loved the world, that he gave his only begotten Son, that whosoever believeth in him should not perish, but have everlasting life.
For God sent not his Son into the world to condemn the world; but that the world through him might be saved.

This seemed to help quiet the hysteria around him. He listened as the flight attendants gave emergency instructions, while wishing he had his own reference to God's emergency instructions.

The pilot prepared them for a crash, but actually was able to make it to the closest airport and land with only one engine.

After landing and departing the plane, the relieved passengers learned it would be several hours before another flight could be prepared for them to continue their trip.

Patrick quietly asked the ticket agent if there was a Bible bookstore in the town they were in. Then he quickly left the airport in a cab.

Always keep the Word of God close to you. We can't see what is ahead for us in any given day. God gave us the Word to prepare us and to help us through this life with all the struggles. Expect the struggles to come on a regular basis.

It's very important to bury the Word in your heart, but it's also very important to always be able to grasp that Bible in your hand and search the scriptures for that one verse that is needed, minute by minute, in the midst of any need or crisis.

Giving All

Carol Bryan constantly amazed everyone that knew her. They always wondered how anyone with all of her problems could do as much as she did and be so spiritually strong.

Carol was crippled from a childhood disease and confined to a wheelchair. She suffered great pain, and battled daily just to exist, yet most people never knew that.

Her eyesight was very poor; she had lost sight in one eye in the accident that took her husband and child. The sight was damaged in the other eye, and she could see very little.

These things certainly didn't hinder her ability as a Sunday school teacher to the young adult class. She rarely missed a Sunday. In addition, she attended the prayer group, served in the choir, and was always available to help others.

She never failed to bring her acclaimed lemon pound cake to every gathering, as well to give one to every bereaved family who had suffered a loss.

Her list of unseen accomplishments was endless in the church, as well as in the community. She always seemed to be the first to volunteer, despite any difficulty in mobility or vision.

Carol didn't like talking about herself, but finally an enterprising young reporter succeeded in convincing her to be interviewed.

Dan began by asking, "Mrs. Bryan, how do you manage to read the Word to prepare for the Sunday lessons as well as the other things you do that require reading?"

Carol looked at him, surprised, "It really isn't a hindrance, Dan. Have you never heard of Braille, large print, magnifiers, or audio CDs of the Bible? Our modern world makes it very easy for sight-impaired people to 'read' what they need to. Even Paul probably had eye problems, because he wrote to the Galatians and mentioned using large letters in **Galatians 6**. He probably had many other infirmities in his body from all the beatings, prison time, stoning and shipwrecks. ***2 Corinthians 11:23-28***.

"But I have to admit, I've committed much of God's Word to memory, beginning many years ago. That is the one thing that keeps me going when other things fail.

"You see, when the Word is memorized and buried in your heart, it is always handy, always ready to be used, and with the enemy constantly coming against you, it is always needed."

2 Timothy 2:15 Study to shew thyself approved unto God, a workman that needeth not to be ashamed, rightly dividing the word of truth.

"But, why do you do so much?" Dan questioned. "You could just sit back and let someone healthier take over. Everyone would certainly understand. You've done so much more than most people do."

"Well, Dan, it's just a matter of following Jesus. We're to live by His example. Jesus lived entirely for others and not for himself. When He gave His life on the Cross for us, he gave everything He had. Everything before the Cross points towards it, and everything since that time points back towards the Cross.

"Can we do any less? If we're to represent Christ to a lost and dying world, we have to give everything we can give. Our cross might not be a wooden cross that takes our life, but we all have some kind of cross to bear. He told us it would be easy to bear as long as we are following Him, and it really is."

Matthew 16:24 Then said Jesus unto his disciples, If any man will come after me, let him deny himself, and take up his cross, and follow me.

Offended: Satan's Trap

1Timothy 4:1 Now the Spirit speaketh expressly, that in the latter times some shall depart from the faith, giving heed to seducing spirits, and doctrines of devils;

"Well, I'll tell you this, I'm not going back in that room. They might fire me, but he is so mean and violent. I think he could easily kill someone.

It's like nothing I've ever seen. There's a heavy blackness that is just evil all around that man," the nurse tossed the chart on the desk. "Most things don't scare me, but I'm afraid to go back in there," she firmly stated.

Heather spoke up, "I'll take care of him, if you'll let me have my break first."

"You've got it, and thank you," Connie gratefully answered.

Heather walked down to the unoccupied linen room where she knew she would have some privacy. She sank to her knees beside the small chair in the corner and began to earnestly seek God.

"Father, I give you all the praise because I know you are with me and will guide me in the care of this patient. You are all-powerful, and all the glory will be yours.

"Father, this very morning you led me to study in **Matthew 16**, and in your Word you said you would give me the keys of the kingdom of Heaven. Those keys are the symbol of power and authority here on this earth.

"I ask that you go before me into that room and counteract any evil, or any power of darkness that may surround that patient."

Heather prayed for the full 30 minutes of her break time. Refreshed and with renewed confidence that Jesus would help her to do whatever was necessary, she picked up the chart and went into the room.

"Hello, Mr. Carter, I am Heather, and I'll be your nurse for this shift. How are you feeling?"

"Well, it's so strange," he hesitantly said, "I actually feel like an entirely different person. It happened just a few minutes ago. Something just overwhelmed me, and it was like a release.

"I've been walking in a kind of blackness for so long, and now I feel like the darkness has lifted. It's.... well you might not understand, but it's like I felt when I got saved and was working in the Lord's will.

"Please don't think I'm crazy, but I've been in that darkness for so long. Most of the time I didn't want to be free from it, but now I'm not so sure," he went on.

Heather finished her tasks and looked directly at him, "I think I do understand, and I think you need to talk to someone about it. Could I contact the hospital chaplain, or do you have a Christian friend or pastor you could call?"

"No, there is no one. If you really think the chaplain could help me, I guess we could try."

A short time later, Bob Douglas knocked and entered John Carter's room. After introductions he said, "Heather mentioned a little about what happened this morning. Is there more you'd like to talk about?"

John told him how he was wonderfully saved in his late teenage years. He transferred to a Bible college to complete his education, and then began to work in the youth group of the church. He married, and everything seemed to go so well. Then someone hurt him, told a lie that really caused a problem in his church work.

"I tried to go to the person, tell the truth of what really happened, but I was so hurt and offended, and it kept eating at me until it was all I could think about.

"I quit working in the church, and then stopped going to church at all. Then I went back to my old ways of living. It destroyed my marriage, and then my Christian life."

"The bitterness and darkness set in, along with drugs, alcohol, and crime of every sort. I can't believe I've never been caught by the police. The car accident is what brought me to the hospital. I think I'll be here for a while with all these injuries."

"John, let's go back to the lie that was told. You should know that to be offended is a trap set by Satan. He lays his trap very carefully, and he feeds that initial offense until it will destroy and pull down a Christian.

"That is his goal. He won't stop until the Christian is totally defeated, or until the person realizes where the attack is coming from and takes authority over the situation.

"There are things one can do when they are offended. I think you tried, but you really didn't try hard enough, and finally gave into the trap Satan had set.

"We'll talk more about that later, but now the most important thing for you is to repent of everything that has happened and put your life back into God's hands. Of course, it's your choice whether to do that or not. It's always your choice; God doesn't force Himself on anyone."

John had tears streaming down his cheeks. "This life will kill me, and I'm so sick of this dark evil that surrounds me. Please pray with me, chaplain."

It was the third day since John turned back to the Lord. Things had dramatically changed in the room. Connie marveled, and didn't mind providing his care at all.

Chaplain Douglas came every day, and today he told John that he wanted to talk more about counteracting the trap that Satan lays for everyone. He brought John a Bible and asked him to turn to **Matthew 14,** starting in verse **22.**

"We've talked about rebuking the enemy and how to do that. Today, we want to talk about something else a Christian can do when the enemy attacks."

Matthew 14:24-32 But the ship was now in the midst of the sea, tossed with waves: for the wind was contrary. And in the fourth watch of the night Jesus went unto them, walking on the sea. And when the disciples saw him walking on the sea, they were troubled, saying, It is a spirit; and they cried out for fear. But straightway Jesus spake unto them, saying, Be of good cheer; it is I; be not afraid. And Peter answered him and said, Lord, if it be thou, bid me come unto thee on the water. And he said, Come. And when Peter was come down out of the ship, he walked on the water, to go to Jesus. But when he saw the wind boisterous, he was afraid; and beginning to sink, he cried, saying, Lord, save me. And immediately Jesus stretched forth his hand, and caught him, and said unto him, O thou of little faith, wherefore didst thou doubt? And when they were come into the ship, the wind ceased.

"John, you know this story, we've all heard it preached numerous times. Let me point out just a couple of things. Jesus sent them to the other side of the sea, which was over thirteen miles away.

"When they were in the middle of the sea, a storm came up. We've all seen how a storm can quickly arise in the midst of a very calm time. Our God always knows when we are in the midst of a storm. We never need to face it alone.

"Jesus walked over six miles on the water, in a storm, to reach them. When they saw Him, they were in such a fearful state, they didn't even recognize him.

"Notice that impetuous Peter was the only one that answered Him when He spoke. But he said....**if**. 'If' usually always denotes doubt. But even doubting, he was the only one of the twelve that ventured out of the boat in that storm.

"Peter definitely had the faith to trust Him and step into the water. We all trust some, but we need to trust with everything we have. Peter took his eyes off Jesus and looked at the storm around him. Of course, he started to sink, but the most important part is that when you cry out to Jesus, He will save you. Do you understand the point of this, John?"

"Yes," John answered, "When Peter took his eyes off of Jesus, he began to sink, just like I sank into the darkness, which was Satan's trap."

"If I had cried out to Jesus to pull me out, He would have. Thank you, Chaplain, I've learned one of the most valuable lessons of my life."

Chapter Ten

Prayer and Supplication

Ephesians 6:18 Praying always with all prayer and supplication in the Spirit, and watching thereunto with all perseverance and supplication for all saints;

    Prayer is not included by Paul with the armor listed in the previous verses. But....prayer is necessary in the Christian's victory over the enemy; therefore it is definitely connected to the weapons used. All of the armor must be put on with prayer.

    Prayer is our connection to the Father who gives the victory. We must have that connection. A well is no good without a bucket, a faucet or a connection with pipes. There has to be a way to reach the flow of the water. Notice how many times the word 'all' is used in the scripture above. It means prayer must be offered constantly and earnestly on every occasion. Every incident in life should be dealt with in prayer.

    Without prayer, there is no power. Power is needed to stand, to lift the shield, to put on the helmet, to wield the sword. The Christian can stand and fight only as long as he remains in the attitude of prayer. We are told to pray 'always' and 'without ceasing'. We need to pray in order to prepare for the battle, as well as in the midst of the fight.

    Prayer is the determining factor in the battle. When the Christian begins to pray, the enemy begins to retreat. Constant discipline is needed to gain power in prayer. The verse tells us to watch with perseverance. This shows the seriousness of the task.

    Without prayer, the armor would not be fully usable. This scripture urges us to pray 'in the Spirit'. Many of us understand that to be praying as the Holy Spirit gives utterance in unknown tongues. There is power in praying in the Spirit.

Often we pray the way we feel we should pray. That might not be the way God would have us to pray. Praying in the Spirit enables us to pray exactly the way we should for each situation.

We're to pray for all Christians. All of us are going through warfare. Compassion and concern for others must be paramount. They are going through the same kind of suffering that we are.

Our prayers bound together with theirs makes for an extremely strong fortress. Two or more praying can put the enemy to flight.

It is also necessary to be constantly alert.

2 Timothy 4:5 But watch thou in all things,...

It's a sad fact that Satan sometimes uses our families and friends to attack us and do his dirty work. If we are not alert, we won't be able to fight properly.

Return from the Battle

The tall, once-handsome soldier moved through the terminal, his duffle bag slung over one shoulder. He limped very noticeably and a ragged scar crossed his cheek down into his neck.

He looked pale, even haggard, a once vigorous young man, now physically ravaged by war. The tortured memories were reflected in his eyes, which were no longer young, but mature far beyond their years. Yet in all this, there was a definite peace about him.

He found a seat at the gate and prepared to wait through the two-hour layover before taking the last flight home. The leave time would be much appreciated before returning to his next duty station.

The older lady sitting next to him touched his shoulder and haltingly said, "Thank you! Thank you for fighting for us."

"It's an honor to serve our country by helping to defend it," he answered sincerely.

They were waiting for the same flight, and spoke at length about fighting and serving in the military. He learned she was an Air Force widow. Her husband was killed in the Korean War. They found they both believed in the importance of prayer to sustain, especially in the difficult times.

He asked her if she also relied on the importance of praise as a part of prayer. "Oh, yes," she answered, "Sometimes praise is the most important part of prayer. It's when we realize just how much He has already done for us and how He will continue to keep us. Then we can completely trust Him to answer our petitions in the way He knows is the best way."

"Remember when Jesus taught the disciples how they should pray in ***Matthew 6,*** and verse ***11.*** *He said...*

'Hallowed be thy name'.'" They were told to praise Him before they were to do anything else. Our example should always be to praise the one who died for us.

Ephesians 3:20,21 Now unto him that is able to do exceeding abundantly above all that we ask or think, according to the power that worketh in us,
 Unto him be glory in the church by Christ Jesus throughout all ages, world without end. Amen.

He listened to her respectfully, and then said, as the tears came to his eyes, "I know you're right, but that's the part I struggle with. 'Praising Him in all things', I saw my friends killed and wounded, little children hurt every day as the innocent victims of war. It can be so hard sometimes to praise Him in these things we can't understand at all."

She responded with compassion, "When we begin our prayers by praising God, He eases our fears and uncertainties immediately. After all, He is in control, and knows what we are praying about before we ever voice our prayer.

Remember we are not praising Him **for** the horrible things that are happening, but we are praising Him **in all things**, showing that we trust Him, no matter what is happening."

"Thank you," he answered, "it's so good to talk to someone who believes the same way I do, and you've increased my faith today by reminding me of things I had forgotten."

She patted his hand, "God loves us and is keeping us through all the things we go through. And in each of these things we will grow as Christians if we rely on Him. You can count on me, son, to keep you in my prayers."

They were called to board their flight, and they both knew they had each found a fellow Christian they could depend on.

Persecution

"But, Granny, you don't understand! They really hate me in that school. All the kids laugh and make fun of me. They make fun of my red hair, my acne, my weight, and especially because I have problems understanding the new subjects.

"They even laugh because they have more privileges than I do. I've never been so miserable. Just because most of them are rich and smart and good looking, they think everyone else is beneath them. Oh, Granny, I want to move back to Richland. I miss my friends.

"Some of these kids are bullies, and they try to push me around, too. They even make fun of me because I'm a Christian. I don't think any of them even go to church. They're mean and awful, and I wish I could get back at them someway. What am I going to do, Granny?" Ellie sobbed.

"Ellie, remember why your parents moved here?" Granny responded. "Having this stroke really disabled me. I couldn't move to your home because all the bedrooms were upstairs.

"Your mom and dad were so kind in moving here to my home so I didn't have to go to a nursing facility. I didn't want to do that, yet. We know how difficult it has been for you here, but the Bible does have a solution if you want me to tell you about it."

"Oh, Granny, I love being here with you, and I'm really glad Dad could get a transfer. It's just those mean kids at school. Yes, please tell me what the Bible says."

"Ellie, this may be painful, but we need to understand this verse." Granny turned in the Bible to **Matthew 5:44** and read it to Ellie.

Matthew 5:44   But I say unto you, Love your enemies, bless them that curse you, do good to them that hate you, and pray for them which despitefully use you, and persecute you;

"You see, Honey, God's Word tells us to do just the opposite of what we want to do. It tells us to love them, and we know just how unlovable they are. It tells us to pray for them, and it doesn't matter if we want to or not, or if we feel like it or not."

"God is able to touch them and give them a different nature. Do you suppose that these children might have problems of their own, and that's why they want to take it out on someone else?" asked Granny.

"Well," Ellie thought, "most of them just live with one parent, instead of two, and I heard some of them talking about parents that drank all the time and wouldn't give them any attention at all. I guess that they could have problems of their own. Maybe you're right, Granny, I'll start to pray for them."

～～～

It is necessary to pray for those who torment, dislike, and persecute us. Otherwise we tend to judge them, and usually judge them unfairly because we only see one side.

It's hard to judge someone when you're asking God to touch them. You'll be more interested in how God will touch them, instead of judging and wanting to pay them back.

Praying Always

Betty had come to stay with Carina while she went through the needed chemotherapy.

At first all went smoothly, and Carina told her, "Mom, you might as well go back home. It looks like this will go very smoothly, and I can handle everything."

"Let's wait and see, Carina. The boys might need more than you're able to do, and with David deployed until next year, it might be best to have someone here for the next few months," Betty replied.

The next several weeks proved that her mom was right. Carina became deathly ill. The nausea was so bad she could rarely eat anything, or even be around food at all.

She stopped trying to drive because she was so weak. She was so thankful her mother was there to manage the boys and take them where they needed to go. Many other things plagued her, like her beautiful, dark hair falling completely out, and extreme numbness in her hands and feet. Sleep seemed to elude her because of the pain, and she was tormented with mouth sores, along with rashes and itching in her body.

"Sorry to interrupt your prayer, can I get you anything, Honey? Do you want to try again to take that anti-nausea medication the doctor prescribed?"

"Thanks, Mom, I better not try it right now. If you would just put that praise CD on, I think I'll just continue praying. Praying for others seems to strengthen and help me more than anything." Carina closed her eyes and concentrated on the needs of others.

Later that day when the pastor came to visit, Betty confided her concerns. "She's very bad physically, Pastor. Several times she had to miss the treatment because of low blood count. The doctors have mentioned hospitalization several times.

"But... spiritually, she is amazing! She seems to pray constantly, and not for herself, but always for the needs of others. She's lifted up all of her family, her friends, everyone in the church, the men in her husband's squadron, all the leaders of our city, state, and country, and all the others going through medical treatments. She says this helps her, but I don't understand."

"Well, Betty, I don't understand either, since I'm not where she is, but I can't help thinking of Job. Hardly anyone had suffered the losses and pain of Job.

"He lost all his children, his sustenance, as well as his health, but he never lost his faith. His wife turned against him, his friends were not friends at all. Job said '*I know my redeemer liveth,*' and even if he were to be destroyed, he said '*in my flesh I shall see God.*' *Job 19:25-27.*

"Thinking of others always helps us to not concentrate so much on ourselves. In her body, she is quite helpless right now, but spiritually, she is living *Ephesians 6:18.* It will help her, and God always strengthens those who turn to Him."

Ephesians 6:18 Praying always with all prayer and supplication in the Spirit, and watching thereunto with all perseverance and supplication for all saints;

Mysteries of God

"Hank!" Kirk called across the store display counter, "I haven't seen you in so long. We miss you in church."

"Um, yeah, it's been a while, Kirk."

"Have you got a minute? I'd really like to talk to you, Hank. It won't take long to have a cup of coffee in the café. Let's just do it."

"Well, okay, I guess so. I've missed you, too," Hank slowly answered.

Seated at the table with their coffee, Kirk began, "I know you had some real rough times, Hank. But we've been friends a long time, and friends can help you get through the hard times."

"Kirk, my son is on death row! He'll be executed within a year. Linda couldn't take it. That heart attack took her life. I lost my job, they foreclosed on the house.

"God didn't answer my prayers, Kirk. No, I've not been in church. Truthfully, I miss that love and peace of God in my life, but now I just can't seem to trust Him anymore."

The tears welled in both men's eyes as Kirk silently prayed about what to say to him.

"Hank, I've had some hard times, too, when I found it very hard to pray and praise God. Perhaps the thing that helped me the most during those times, and I know it's helped others, too, was the book of Job. Remember, he lost everything, his children, all his wealth, his health. It was so bad; he wished he had never been born."

"Sometimes God allows Satan to test us with adversity in order to purify us. In everything that happened, Job said **'blessed be the name of the Lord'**, *Job 1:21*. Even his friends turned against him, but Job remained firm."

Job 13:15 Though he slay me, yet will I trust in him....

Kirk continued, "God never told Job why he was suffering. He never gave him a reason. In the end God blessed him more than He did in the beginning, but He never let him know why.

"Hank, we're told to pray and praise God even when He doesn't answer. We can't let the mysteries of God destroy us.

"It's enough to know that He does have a reason, and he knows the end, and what will happen. We have to just continue on and try and be what He wants us to be.

"Please know, Hank, your church family loves you, we are praying for you, and we will support you however we can. You're not alone in this. God is there, He never turned away from you. Just trust Him."

Hank rose up from the chair; with a low "Thanks", he turned and walked away.

Chapter Eleven

On the Run

Through that long, dark night, Taylor continued to walk, and often ran. Her resolve never wavered. She just wanted to get away.

At home, her dad was always drunk, and her stepmom just used her as a slave. There was constant fighting. Taylor was so sick of taking the abuse. She felt the only option was to get away. She was sure they would be glad to get rid of her.

There was little traffic on the road to Fairfield. She ducked into the woods when she saw lights coming. She was tired and thought she had better find a place to rest before daylight. The only plan in her mind was to get away. She didn't think they would bother to look for her, but if they did, she wanted to be sure they didn't find her.

It was better when she had school as a place to get away, but they made her quit school at sixteen. Her stepmom said she'd never amount to anything anyway, so she might as well stay at home. Because her dad used all his income to buy liquor, she and her stepmom took in ironing. It was all they had to live on.

Taylor knew she wasn't attractive, and she had never been able to fix up her hair and wear makeup like most girls. Now at seventeen, she was skinny and boyish-looking. She slipped into an open bathroom at a gas station and looked into the mirror.

She knew it was dangerous for a girl to be on the road alone. She pulled out the pair of scissors in her bag and cut her hair very short.

Yes, it would work, with the baggy jeans and loose shirt and jacket, and the baseball cap; she looked very much like a boy. She wanted to stay on the road until she was several states away.

Taylor had taken what she felt was her part of the ironing money. She hoped that would be enough to buy food until she was far away.

Behind the gas station she noticed some junked cars. Taylor climbed up into the cab of an old truck and wearily went to sleep. The next day she kept heading south, sticking to the smaller roads and the woods.

Several days later, approaching a large city late in the afternoon, a thunderstorm came up and Taylor looked for a shelter to wait out the storm.

She saw an old building a short way off of the road. It was about to fall down, but it had some of the roof still covering it. Gratefully, she sat down in a dry corner. Taylor took out an apple and chunk of cheese she had purchased earlier and began to eat.

"Hey, kid, what you doing here?" Two rough looking men ran into the old shelter just as the rain began to fall much heavier. "You got anything else to eat?"

Taylor shared what she had. "How about cash, you got any money on you?" She knew she needed money but she also knew they would kill her in a minute, and worse, if they discovered she was a girl.

Her mom used to tell her about Jesus and how He protects the people who love Him. It had been a long time since she had thought about that. Silently, she prayed, 'Jesus, if anyone ever needed protection, I do right now. Please help me.'

Reluctantly she pulled out her wallet and emptied the contents, even the change that was in her pocket.

Greedily they grabbed the few bills. "Now get on out of here, we don't need no kid bothering us."

Taylor grabbed her bag and gladly went out into the stormy afternoon. Broke, yes, but they hadn't even hit her, and she was grateful for that.

Taylor moved steadily toward the south. She knew it would be warmer there in the winter months if she was still homeless. Others on the road were moving in that direction, and she was very careful to try and avoid any other confrontations. She knew she was no match for the stronger people that lived on the road, moving from place to place.

Occasionally she managed to work for someone and earn a day's wages. It was enough to keep her going. Often people told her she was just too scrawny, and not strong enough to do the work, but she still felt it was safer to look like a boy than a girl.

There were always dangers and problems on the road. One morning after finding shelter in someone's barn, she woke up violently ill. She tried to get up, knowing that she needed to move on quickly before the family arose and found her, but she was just too sick. She kept coughing uncontrollably. Her head hurt so violently and the barn seemed to be spinning around her.

Helplessly, she lay there moaning. A lady entered the barn to get the chicken food and found her. "Well, who are you, young man?" When she realized how sick this person was, she ran to the house for medicine and supplies.

Taylor thought she had never tasted anything as good as that orange juice and the water the lady kept urging her to drink.

"I'm sorry to be such a bother," Taylor murmured weakly, "I'll be on my way in just a few minutes."

"No, I don't think so, son. You're pretty sick, and that fever is high. I'd take you in the house, but I can't lift you, and my husband is working in town this week. See if you can eat a little bit of these scrambled eggs."

All through that day and the next day, the lady brought her homemade soups and gave her medicine for the fever and the cough. She brought her a pillow and blankets to make her more comfortable in the hay. She constantly sang as she worked, songs like 'Amazing Grace', 'Jesus Loves Me', and 'He Set Me Free.'

As Taylor recovered, she pondered the meaning of these songs, wondering if they could possibly have meaning for her. On the third day, when she felt so much better, she asked Mrs. Cunningham, "Why have you done so much for me? You could have just called the police; you didn't have to help me. I'm so worthless, how could you possibly care for me?"

"Honey, you're no more worthless than I am." In caring for her, Mrs. Cunningham had quickly discovered she was a girl. "Jesus loves each and every one of us, and we're supposed to try and follow His example."

John 15:12 *This is my commandment, That ye love one another, as I have loved you.*

Although Mrs. Cunningham wanted her to stay, and said she would try and find help for her, Taylor knew they were a real poor family, and felt she had better keep moving.

"Remember, Taylor, Jesus loves you, and He'll keep on protecting you, but you need to turn to him and give Him control over your life," Mrs. Cunningham called as Taylor walked away.

A few nights later, Taylor found shelter in a pecan grove. She awoke to find a large rattlesnake not four feet from her face. Carefully, she scooted further away. She pondered the words of Mrs. Cunningham, about Jesus protecting her.

Another day she came face to face with a ferocious raccoon. When she saw the animal showing aggression and making a terrible whining noise she knew it must be sick. She backed away. He appeared disoriented, and finally moved in the other direction.

In all of these things she remembered the line to the song Mrs. Cunningham sang... 'Thru many dangers, toils and snares, I have already come, 'Tis grace that bro't me safe thus far, and grace will lead me home.'

One morning, her attention was drawn to a small country church. There were people gathered and entering. She thought it must be Sunday. Normally, she tended to avoid people, but this time she was drawn closer and closer. Carefully she moved from the woods to the outside wall where she could hear what was going on inside.

She had never been in a church that she could remember. Even though she knew it was dangerous to stay there, she just couldn't leave.

After the singing, which sounded so beautiful to her ears, she heard a voice say, "Turn to I Peter 1, and we'll talk about our wonderful inheritance.

1 Peter 1:4 To an inheritance incorruptible, and undefiled, and that fadeth not away, reserved in heaven for you,

It sounded just about too good to believe. Taylor believed it was just for those people inside. It could never be for her. The preacher went on with more scripture.

1 Peter 1:18-25 Forasmuch as ye know that ye were not redeemed with corruptible things, as silver and gold, from your vain conversation received by tradition from your fathers;
But with the precious blood of Christ, as of a lamb without blemish and without spot:
Who verily was foreordained before the foundation of the world, but was manifest in these last times for you,
Who by him do believe in God, that raised him up from the dead, and gave him glory; that your faith and hope might be in God.

Seeing ye have purified your souls in obeying the truth through the Spirit unto unfeigned love of the brethren, see that ye love one another with a pure heart fervently:
 Being born again, not of corruptible seed, but of incorruptible, by the word of God, which liveth and abideth for ever.
For all flesh is as grass, and all the glory of man as the flower of grass. The grass withereth, and the flower thereof falleth away:
But the word of the Lord endureth for ever. And this is the word which by the gospel is preached unto you.

Taylor had never heard anything like this. She was astounded, and tried to listen carefully to everything this man spoke of. The pastor began to give the invitation, and one of the men went out the door.

"Hi, there," the tall stranger came around to the side of the church, "I'm Jim. Would you like to come inside with us?"

Taylor grabbed her duffle bag and ran towards the woods. "Uh... No, thanks," she mumbled as she ran away. "I'm just passing through. I didn't mean any harm." It was a while before she stopped running.

She couldn't stop thinking about what she had heard. Could it be true? Would Jesus have loved her so much that He gave his life for her? No one ever loved her that much. The preacher had spoken about repenting of sins and accepting Jesus, but she wasn't sure how to do that.

Taylor finally came to one of the largest cities in the south. Instead of avoiding it, she went right into it. She hoped to find work and a place to stay, but didn't know how to go about it. The day before, she had washed her clothes and bathed in a small creek she had found in some deep woods. She still didn't feel very presentable for the task of searching for work.

Her few attempts at finding work were not successful. She didn't even have an address or a phone number to put down on the two applications she filled out. It seemed kind of lame to say 'Well, I'll just check back with you in a few days,' but that's what she had to do when they asked how they could contact her.

Darkness was falling, and she was in the middle of the city. She had already been asked to move on out of the park she found. She decided to keep walking until she could find some place to stay for the night. She stuck to the shadows and tried to avoid other people on the street.

Hours later and on the verge of exhaustion, she saw them, a group of four young people approaching her. She realized she had been spotted, and it was too late to run.

"You're new around here. You got drugs? Or money," one of them asked. She shook her head. "Check the bag, Doug. Come on, kid, empty your pockets."

Taylor showed her empty pockets while Doug rifled through her bag.

"I guess he's clean. We've got 'ice', you want some?" The girl asked.

Taylor knew they were speaking of the drug known as crystal meth. Again she shook her head. She decided she had nothing to lose by asking for help, so she ventured. "Where do you stay? I've been walking all day, and need a place to spend the night."

After a little discussion, they agreed Taylor could go with them to their camp. They cut through some alleyways and suddenly they were out of town and in a wooded section. On the way, they explained the rules of the camp: no stealing from each other, share whatever they came up with, and since two of them were underage, be careful not to lead the cops to their camp.

Taylor was eighteen, but she wanted no confrontation with law enforcement, and she gratefully agreed to abide by their rules.

The next day, Taylor talked to Doug and Hannah. Roger and Dave were still high on drugs. Doug and Hannah told Taylor they lived mostly on 'spangling'. They stood in front of a store and asked for spare change, until someone chased them off.

Both of them admitted they had sometimes resorted to 'survival sex', which was selling their bodies. Doug told how these older guys really preferred young guys to girls. Roger made money off of drug-running, and Dave often stole things to get by.

Tears came to Taylor's eyes. "I just want to get work and find a place of my own." They admitted they would like to get out of it, too, but people didn't hire street kids. Many were addicts like Roger and Dave. Hannah was an alcoholic and really didn't want to change. It was the only way she could forget the pain of her life.

"There's got to be some way out!" Taylor exclaimed.

"Well, there is the group home, but you have to get accepted for it, and there's a long list." explained Doug.

"We do get to go to the mission once every thirty days. They let us stay five nights, with beds and three meals a day. It's really good; you have to leave in the daytime, and you have to go to their church service every night, but it's not so bad.

"You have to stay clean while you're there, no drugs or drinking, but it's so good to have a bed, shower and meals. Even Hannah, Roger and Dave can make it for five days.

I think it's being homeless that drives them to the drugs and alcohol." Doug went on. "We can go back to the mission in five days, you'll like it there. We'll go out this afternoon and show you where to apply for the group home."

That afternoon, Taylor found a job scrubbing the windows and sweeping the parking lot of a convenience store. She bought food and shared what she had with the others at the camp.

Taylor knew she needed to tell the others that she was a girl instead of a guy before they went to the mission, but it seemed she could pick up a little more work dressed as a guy. She did tell them that night, and it really didn't make any difference to them.

In the next few days, Taylor picked up a little work and always shared with the others what she had. Looking around on the streets, she realized how great it was that her group had accepted her. There was so much danger out there. Doug warned her to stay close to them, as there were so many pedophiles, and pimps, and others all looking for fresh new faces. She again felt like there was someone protecting her.

People, for the most part, hated and shunned them. Only those stronger and meaner would approach and try and take advantage of them.

One night, Taylor gave in and drank with her friends when Hannah brought a bottle into their camp. She found it was true, it did make you forget the pain of your life, but Taylor hated the pull of the alcohol, and knew she could fall into the trap and soon would depend on it. She vowed never to touch it again, and to just keep searching for a permanent way out of her situation.

When the day came that they could go to the mission, they happily headed down to the street where it was located. They filled out the papers and were given their bed assignments.

Taylor had removed her cap and registered as a girl to be included in the women's dorm. Her hair was beginning to grow out and frame her face nicely. It was so nice to have a hot shower. They had even been taken to the clothing closet and allowed to pick out clean clothing.

The hot meal was wonderful. After that, they gathered in the recreation room for the nightly service. This was the part Taylor looked forward to the most. She just had to know more about this person, Jesus, who she kept hearing about.

Every night they had different speakers, all volunteers from various churches. Sometimes they sang and played instruments. Every night they spoke about Jesus. Jesus, who raised the dead, healed the sick, gave his life for sinners, and would never leave those who turned their lives over to Him.

The fourth night, the speaker spoke of the protection God gives us. He told how Satan provides dens and caves that have only one way in and one way out. You can hide a little while, but then you come back out into sin again. Then he spoke of how God provides tunnels and goes through them with us to the other end of the problem.

He spoke of the weapons given the Christian to fight with. But most of all, how He is always with us, helping, guiding, and carrying us through the bad times.

Ephesians 6:13-18 Wherefore take unto you the whole armour of God, that ye may be able to withstand in the evil day, and having done all, to stand.
Stand therefore, having your loins girt about with truth, and having on the breastplate of righteousness;
And your feet shod with the preparation of the gospel of peace;
Above all, taking the shield of faith, wherewith ye shall be able to quench all the fiery darts of the wicked.
And take the helmet of salvation, and the sword of the Spirit, which is the word of God:
Praying always with all prayer and supplication in the Spirit, and watching thereunto with all perseverance and supplication for all saints;

Suddenly it all made sense to Taylor. She understood how He loved her so much, and she didn't want to go on without repenting and accepting Jesus. With tears rolling down her face, Taylor went to the front when the altar call was given and prayed that God would forgive her sins and be with her forever.

After the service, Taylor and her friends sat together at one of the dining tables. "What are you going to do now?" asked Hannah, "It would be really hard for a Christian to live on the streets with us. You probably feel like you're too good for us now."

"Oh, no," Taylor answered, "You'll always be my friends, even if I can find a way to get off of the streets. Tomorrow is our last day here. I guess I'll continue to stay with you until I can find a job.

"I wish you could feel the love and peace I feel inside of me right now. It's like nothing I've ever felt before. I just know without a doubt, Jesus will continue to take care of me and make a way out of this trouble."

"I don't know, Taylor, my folks were supposed to be Christians, but when I got on drugs, they kicked me out and told me never to come back. They didn't even try to help." Dave shook his head. "I just don't think that's the life for me."

The next day, Mr. Summers, the director of the mission, pulled Taylor aside and asked, "Taylor, I need someone to stay at the front desk and help sort the clothing that comes in. Would you be interested in staying here permanently?"

"The pay isn't great, but you get free room and board. You have to be completely clean from drugs and alcohol, but I don't think you have a problem with that."

"Oh, thank you so much. I'll do a good job for you," Taylor responded with tears in her eyes.

Taylor did work very hard and stayed at the mission two years, taking college courses when she could. Then she moved to a better job and her own apartment. She is very involved with her church, and is dating a young man who is called into the mission field. They met at the mission when he was one of the regulars who came to lead the nightly services. Now they both devote one night a week to go to the mission and volunteer.

She continued to see her friends, especially on the five days a month when they came to the mission. Dave went to the altar and gave his life to Christ a few months after Taylor did. He and Roger were accepted into a group home, and they both found jobs and moved back into the world.

Hannah disappeared one night and never came back to the camp. They never found out what happened to her.

Doug remains on the street, and has no desire to do anything else. He remains good friends with Taylor, Dave and Roger.

After two years, Taylor wrote a long letter to her dad and stepmother. She shared with them the joy and happiness that she found when she accepted Christ. She assured them that she had forgiven them for any wrong or mistreatment she had suffered while she was with them. She gave them her address, but didn't hear back from them.

Author's Note

Dear readers, Thank you! I am humbled and honored that you would choose to read this narrative. Throughout the years, I've personally fought many battles, some are still ongoing, and new ones show up daily.

I've witnessed joy, sorrow, hurt, heartbreak, physical pain, the empty happiness the world offers, as well as the fulfilling contentment and peace that God gives.

In all this, it's clear that my God is the same as the God of...

2 Corinthians 1:3,4 ....the Father of our Lord Jesus Christ, the Father of mercies, and the God of all comfort; Who comforteth us in all our tribulation, that we may be able to comfort them which are in any trouble,..........

I pray that this book will offer you some insight or measure of comfort as you move through this battlefield of earthly life in preparation to enter into life eternal with the Lord.

While writing, I often thought perhaps this book applies only to me. The battles have been much more heated during this time of study, research and writing. I have learned and re-learned throughout. Old truths have become new, and have been urgently applied to current battles.

Yet, I realize this book must also apply to others, not just me. God so specifically directed me to record these words. When an old warrior learns and gleans, it is often to help others that through study and prayer they could also apply these truths. When we stop learning, we begin to die, just as everything in nature.

An interesting side-note comes from the study and exploration of the rise and fall of the Roman Empire. We know Paul's description was based upon his firsthand knowledge and observation of the soldier's garb. In the ensuing centuries, many things led to the downfall of the Roman Empire, including the rise of Christianity, corrupt political and cultural elements, economic turmoil, and prolonged, expensive wars.

Many military soldiers had a reputation for incompetence and cowardice. The leaders became convinced the armor needed to be updated. Some believed the full armor was just too heavy. The armor evolved into a more fashionable and lightweight style. It's true that it was easier to wear, but also much easier for the enemies' weapons to penetrate in battles.

More and more battles were lost. Was this indeed perhaps one of the causes for the decline and fall of the empire? It is certainly an interesting thought.

Have you ever felt that the armor weighs more than you want to carry? If you have, think harder, my friend, on the possible effects of not putting this armor on. It's really lightweight compared to the heaviness of the sin burden that so many carry. The benefits of its protection far outweigh any discomfort of wearing it daily.

It all seems to come down to separation from the world and standing for Christ. You cannot belong to both. There has to be a choice. At birth, we come into this world belonging to Satan, with the sin nature built in. Jesus is the only one who can change this nature by forgiving sin. The Christian is one who has accepted Christ and desires to follow him.

Christ desires that Christians be separate from the world and holy unto Him. **Numbers 6:8**. That holiness only comes when we fight in the battles, the battles which separate Christians from the world.

This writing perhaps might seem severe and dwell on the hardship of being a good soldier.

Acts 20:24 But none of these things move me, neither count I my life dear unto myself, so that I might finish my course with joy, and the ministry, which I have received of the Lord Jesus, to testify the gospel of the grace of God

Never forget the tremendous joy and rewards that are also reserved for the one who finishes his course. Yes, the soldier's life is full of danger, fighting, suffering, great pain, and heartbreak, but all of this is nothing compared to the joy at the final victory. Hold to that promise and fight on tirelessly.

This was written with a heart full of love, prayers, and compassion for your struggles, my fellow soldiers in the battle.

If you've not yet committed your life to Christ, perhaps you will see that the joy of what is ahead for Christians far outweighs the battles we fight here, and make that commitment before Jesus returns to take the Christians home forever.

Saved or unsaved, this life is a battlefield with one major difference. Christians don't fight alone. In or out of battles, we depend on:

….the Father of mercies, and the God of all comfort
2 Corinthians 1:3b

Jean Mallory, author and free-lance writer, was born in a small town in New Mexico. She has traveled extensively and now makes her home in north Florida.

The mother of three daughters, she is also a grandmother and great-grandmother. Widowed since 1989, Jean is still active in managing her small business.

She has authored free-lance articles and created curriculum in her church. She has taught Sunday school, and teaches Christian financial affairs in outreach ministries. 'Weapons for the Battlefield' is her second book.

www.ingramcontent.com/pod-product-compliance
Lightning Source LLC
Chambersburg PA
CBHW032358040426
42451CB00006B/48